Praise for *Garden of Bliss*

"Everyone has a secret garden, but few of us are aware of it. That's why it's secret. By inviting you into her garden, Debra Moffitt uncovers and unlocks the gate to your own. This is a book for the spiritual gardener eager to till the soil of self and harvest the wisdom of Self."

—Rabbi Rami Shapiro, author of *Writing, The Sacred Art* and columnist for *Spirituality & Health Magazine*

"If you are feeling depleted and spent, Debra Moffitt gently guides you to your inner space to refresh and inspire a serene state of joy, awakening, and creativity. *Garden of Bliss* is a must-read in today's harried world. I keep it on my bedside table to read again and again."

—Mary Alice Monroe, *New York Times* bestselling author of *Beach House Memories*

"For those of us who suffer status anxiety, Debra Moffitt shows how to let go of the constant chattering thoughts of want. She gives us a formula for introspection, peace, and love that can't be bought at any price. *Garden of Bliss* is the story of the birth of a writer, but also a lesson on how to step out of the rat race and take stock of what's really important in life ... Like *Eat, Pray, Love* without the whine!"

—Janna McMahan, bestselling author of *Anonymity* and *The Ocean Inside*

"A lushly detailed, luxuriant read of a book, brimming with tales of Moffitt's world travels as soul awakening. Readers are invited to embark upon their own soul journey using dreaming, intuition, and synchronicity, and to enter the secret garden of their inner world for extraordinary healing and growth. Highly recommended!"

—Sara Wiseman, author of *Becoming Your Best Self* and *Writing the Divine*

"*Garden of Bliss* is a must-read, a keeper that will enhance your personal library, a book that you will refer to again and again along your spiritual path. Written from a personal perspective with engaging accounts and innovative methods for connecting to your own inner gardener, Debra Moffitt has written a work of pure inspiration. If you want to live a purposeful life, *Garden of Bliss* will show you how to tend your inner garden so that your soul blooms with divine joy."

— Melissa Alvarez, author of *365 Ways to Raise Your Frequency*

"This is a wonderfully courageous, open, poetic work of soul exploration. Debra guides the reader on the winding pathway of her own soul discovery with vivid, soul-shaping incidents punctuated by equally powerful dreams and inspirations. Here is a record, rare and precious, of authentic spiritual discovery in the Hermetic sense: the soul's thirst for worthiness and meaning initiated through real-life events, persons, and inner manifestations results in the creation and cultivation of an alchemical 'secret garden.' The distillations of that garden find expression in practices, dream guidance, visualizations, and multiple techniques, all of which point toward self-discovery and soul awakening. Love is the watchword; feminine wisdom, the light; and storied narrative, the music. A valuable, intelligent, soulful book."

— Dr. Lee Irwin, Professor of Religious Studies, College of Charleston, and author of *Alchemy of Soul: The Art of Spiritual Transformation*

About the Author

Debra Moffitt is an award-winning author and teacher devoted to nurturing the spiritual in everyday life. She leads workshops on spiritual practices in the United States and Europe and is a faculty member of the Esalen Institute and the Sophia Institute. Her mind/body/spirit articles, essays, and stories appear in publications around the globe. She has spent over fifteen years practicing meditation, working with dreams, and doing spiritual practices. She resides in South Carolina and Europe.

Visit her online at www.debramoffitt.com. You can also e-mail her at dm@debramoffitt.com.

Garden of Bliss

Cultivating the Inner Landscape
for Self-Discovery

DEBRA MOFFITT

Llewellyn Publications
Woodbury, Minnesota

First Edition
First Printing, 2013

Book design by Donna Burch
Cover design by Lisa Novak
Cover image: Birds on branches: iStockphoto.com/Eli Griffith
Cover lettering illustration: Alison Carmichael/Jelly
Interior birds from Art Explosion

Llewellyn Publications is a registered trademark of Llewellyn Worldwide Ltd.

Library of Congress Cataloging-in-Publication Data
Moffitt, Debra, 1961–
   Garden of bliss : cultivating the inner landscape for self-discovery / Debra Moffitt.
      pages   cm
   ISBN 978-0-7387-3382-1
1. Spirituality—Miscellanea. 2. Spiritual life—Miscellanea. I. Title.
   BF1999.M726 2013
   204'.4—dc23
                              2012047465

Llewellyn Worldwide Ltd. does not participate in, endorse, or have any authority or responsibility concerning private business transactions between our authors and the public.
   All mail addressed to the author is forwarded, but the publisher cannot, unless specifically instructed by the author, give out an address or phone number.
   Any Internet references contained in this work are current at publication time, but the publisher cannot guarantee that a specific location will continue to be maintained. Please refer to the publisher's website for links to authors' websites and other sources.

Llewellyn Publications
A Division of Llewellyn Worldwide Ltd.
2143 Wooddale Drive
Woodbury, MN 55125-2989
www.llewellyn.com

Printed in the United States of America

Also by this author

Awake in the World: 108 Practices to Live a Divinely Inspired Life

Riviera Stories

For all of the seeking souls—
may you find joy in your
secret garden of bliss.

Contents

Part Three—Tending the Secret Garden

Part Four—Harvesting the Joy

Awakening

No hurry or worry.
The secret garden will reawaken
and blossom at the right time.
Be prepared to dig.

The garden is a metaphor for life,
and gardening is a symbol of the spiritual path.
—LARRY DOSSEY

Introduction

The Secret Garden: A Gateway to Reviving the Feminine Spirit and Finding Bliss

A few years ago I lived on the French Riviera and worked in international business. I lived in a sea-view apartment filled with French antiques, beautiful oriental rugs, and designer furniture. One evening while friends sat with my French husband around the Louis Philippe mahogany table clinking crystal glasses filled with Château Margaux, I stood in the kitchen staring out at Venus rising over the sea beyond the luxury yachts. From the outside looking in, my life appeared perfect. I had plenty of things: money, a good job. I met rock stars and millionaires. And none of it mattered.

A deep emptiness gnawed at me. The things that I bought no longer satisfied the hunger in my heart. A sense of despair descended, and it contrasted with the laughter bubbling up from the dining room. If this is all there is, I thought, then I might as well climb up on the windowsill and jump out. Because I don't care. I don't care about having more money. I don't care about more things or more superficial relationships. If this is all that life offers, then I'm stepping out.

I calculated how easy it would be to pull a chair next to the windowsill, climb up, and simply allow my body to fall four stories to the street. Then an inner voice broke in, "There's something more. Go find it."

"What?" I said. The despair brought an opening, a space where the ego-self was on its knees and my soul-Self, that divine spark within, could speak and be heard. "Go find it," it said. Instead of wasting a life, I listened and immediately set out to discover what might make life beautiful and meaningful, and set my soul on fire. It started with another kind of leap, a leap of faith. Even though I traveled all over the world on business, I feared flying. I also feared leaving the job that shackled me to a way of life that consumed my spirit. "If I can leap out of a plane, then I can leave that job and write," I decided. As a child I'd always dreamed of writing. Why not commit to it and begin?!

When I found myself strapped to a French parachuter free-falling from 14,000 feet above St. Tropez, the exhilaration of leaping into a new life ripped through my veins, and a few months after that ritual leap the universe conspired to release me from the corporate job with a "golden parachute." With savings and time to explore the inner world, my dreams activated and a series of synchronicities arose that opened doors to the realm of the spirit. In Europe this realm is often mysteriously called the secret garden. Secret gardens thrive within us. They're places of the spirit and imagination where we can rediscover peace and grow into who we are. In them our souls communicate with us using the language of symbols. It's the way the soul-Self dances around the mind to show us another path, one that allows mystery and a profound connection with the Divine Feminine.

Garden of Bliss reveals the process of soul growth—the way intuition, dreams, and insights expand and guide us when we dare to go inside the secret garden of the soul and get to work. It's a companion to my first book, *Awake in the World: 108 Practices to Live a Divinely Inspired Life*, which grew out of my journey into the secret garden, and it responds to readers who wanted to know more of the story behind the scenes. Some names and details in this book have been changed at the editor's request to respect individual privacy and for the flow of the story, but it essentially reflects my experiences of waking up to the inner life of the spirit.

By sharing my story as I cultivated my inner secret garden of the soul, I hope to inspire you to explore your spirit and tend it as well. Many of you feel the call of your spirits nudging you to make authentic inner changes that lead to big changes in the world. We're being called to find jobs, partners, and creative expressions, and to engage in life in ways that nourish our spirits and create harmony. I believe that the more of us who do this, the better and more peaceful the world will become. From this inner place of peace and bliss we can truly make contributions that make the world a better place.

Secret gardens are symbols that hold mystical, symbolic properties which reflect the inner secrets of the soul. These hidden gardens appeared across Europe during the chaotic, crazy, and violent times of the Middle Ages as spaces for healing and refuge. Delicate, beautiful jasmine, roses, healing herbs, and trees that could not grow outside in the madness could take root here and flourish. Like *The Secret Garden* book by Frances Hodgson Burnett, which was also inspired by these ancient European legends, the garden is a place that heals our relationships with others, with Mother Nature, and most importantly, with our own spirits. When we rediscover the path, relocate the key, and cross over the threshold into it, we find peace and stillness, a place where potential waits to be crystalized and turned into form. This protected place opens up dreams, plants seeds of ideas, and allows projects to take shape and your soul to grow behind walls far from judgmental eyes. Tending it regularly ultimately leads to bliss.

The process of conscious soul growth that happens when you cross the threshold into this sacred interior is one that goes through natural cycles of preparation, clearing, planting, growth, tending, and harvesting. The book is divided into sections that focus on these different phases of tending and cultivating the inner landscape of the soul. As you read through the chapters, the story is filled with travels from France to India, but it's not necessary to cross the globe to develop your relationship with your spirit. All you have to do is dare to step inside and spend some time with your soul-Self—the wise, inner gardener of your spirit—and the adventure begins. If you're inclined to seek the support of a friend, the exercises at the end of the chapters can be fun and rewarding to do with others.

If you choose to take the journey into your secret garden, a world of adventure opens into your sacred inner place of wisdom. In this place you can discover and develop gifts, abilities, and a connection with the Divine that will sustain you and allow you to grow a life that becomes more rewarding, meaningful, and creative. It's a place where you can begin to connect with your natural gifts of intuition, vision, and insight, and use them in your work and daily life for guidance. Dreams and symbols become powerful allies. Synchronicity and flow will become your natural state of being. You'll renew your connection with your true nature of peace and from this place open up to the Source of creative energy. The secret garden can help you to reconnect with the best and highest places in your Self and soar into unique expressions of your true nature. It eventually transforms into a garden of bliss, where the spirit blooms constantly with fragrant flowers of joy and light shines abundantly.

In *Journey into the Secret Garden* workshops at venues in the United States and Europe, from the Esalen Institute in Big Sur, California, to the Sophia Institute in Charleston, South Carolina, and beyond, I encourage women and men to deepen contact with their soul-Self by helping them to learn the language of their souls and connect with their innate creativity and intuition. Some of the exercises from the workshops are included here at the end of the chapters to encourage you to reflect on your inner landscape and consciously cultivate it. While your way into your secret garden may be different from mine, I hope that the exercises will act as springboards to encourage you to plunge into the deep waters of your spirit and discover a way that works for you.

The secret garden is a protected place where you can experiment with changes, transform ways that no longer serve you, learn to tame your mind, connect with emotions, and trust your insights. It's a place to regain your feminine power and thrive. You'll return with the rich harvest of a more meaningful life, greater peace, and contentment. Opening up the gate, and entering inside, promises contact with the power of the human spirit. When we face the inner demons and work to clear away junk that may lurk inside, it brings healing and wholeness. In the beginning it is enough to simply dare to step inside and explore. Open the gate, cross the threshold, and let's begin.

Part One

Breaking New Ground

To grow, the seed needs to be
dropped in dirt and covered in darkness,
and to struggle to reach the light.

A secret garden implies that you do not know what you are going to find—an enclosure hidden from view until the last moment. Open the gate and suddenly all is revealed.

—ROBIN COMPTON

Chapter 1

Finding the Secret Garden

Secret gardens pop up casually in conversations in Europe. If you're in France, someone may suggest that you ponder a big life decision in your "jardin secret." In Italy they'll urge you to go into your "giardino segreto" as a way to discover what you really want and feel. It's a symbolic way of referring to that wonderful, little-known, and mysterious inner place of the soul that holds answers to who we really are and what we really desire. Rediscovering it (for it has always been there) ignites a renewed sense of excitement and childlike playfulness. The long-awaited journey starts. The synchronicities begin, and if you're open to it, life becomes a series of adventurous, mystical, and unexpected encounters that lead you right to where you need to be.

This happened to me as I stood in the garden at a party in Grasse, the perfume capital of the world, located in the South of France. I met a perfumer with a sixth sense. "You must learn to cultivate your *jardin secret*," he whispered. As a "nose," he said that he spent most of his time in front of a thousand bottles set up to look like an organ. I'd just confessed that my French husband had moved out and I'd just left my high-paying executive job to start a new life. I admitted that despite all of the material things I owned I felt empty and longed for a more meaningful life. He said I'd find it in a secret garden.

"*Un jardin secret*," I said. "Do I have one?"

"Ah," he said with a Provençal accent and sniffed the air. "Everybody has one. The Italians have them. Americans like you must have them, too."

"You're not talking about a physical place," I said.

"*Mais non*. It's inside you." He pointed at my chest.

He explained to me that secret gardens sprang up in the Dark Ages, that chaotic, war-and-plague-infested period when things could only grow hidden away behind protected walls. It was a time when political power struggles, drought, and famine left people struggling for survival. Those gardens reflected inner, sacred places of the soul. If you dare to enter inside, it's possible to explore the spiritual realm and grow protected from the harsh eyes, criticisms, and threats of the material world. These feminine places allow intuition, dreams, and insights to come alive.

"You'll be taking a trip soon?" he said.

"No. I hadn't planned on it," I said.

"But your job just ended?"

"Yes," I said.

"When you start the journey, go see my friend." He wrote an address on the back of his card. "He will help you discover more."

I read the name and address aloud. "Karim. In Cairo? Cairo, France?"

His eyes sparkled. "In Egypt. He owns a boutique near the foot of the Great Pyramids of Giza. Very talented perfumer," he said.

"I've always wanted to travel there," I said. "But I can't imagine going...especially not now." Terrorists had attacked and killed a group of tourists only weeks before.

He listened attentively. "We'll see," he said.

"I've been looking for you," the hostess said. She grabbed his elbow and guided him away. He turned and winked at me as he disappeared into an inner garden.

A few weeks later, when I'd forgotten about the conversation, a friend called full of excitement. "I'm going to Egypt. Want to come? Now that you're out of your job, you're free to roam." Maybe most people don't need to lose almost everything and fall into crisis to begin seeking meaning and spiritual connection, but that's what happened to me.

"I should stay here and look for a new job," I said.

"They gave you a good severance package. You can take a break. Come."

I was about to say "no" when the strange secret-garden conversation popped into mind along with the perfumer's predictions.

"I know you've got plenty of miles for a free ticket," Julie said.

"Do you know any noses in Grasse?" I felt perplexed. "Did you tell anyone?" My business experience and practical side made me skeptical of clairvoyants or things that couldn't be explained with reason and deduction.

"I didn't know I was going until yesterday. What's a 'nose' anyway?"

"Oh, someone who creates perfumes."

On the plane, I fished out the card with the perfumer's name on it. "This man, Angelo, gave me his friend's name. Just in case I traveled to Cairo. I thought he was mad," I said.

"Not mad, but psychic maybe. There are no coincidences, you know," she said.

I looked at her, surprised. "Really? Do you know anything about secret gardens?" The engine droned and the puffy clouds vibrated with light beyond the oval window.

"The French talk about them. It's a symbol, I guess," she said.

"They used to exist as real gardens and some still do. But what do you mean by a symbol?"

"Let me see." She bit the tip of her pen and reflected. "It's something in here that connects you to the soul." She pointed to her chest. "A place separated from the usual world. Protected. Things can grow here in secret and become healthy and whole without anyone interfering."

"I think you must have one," I said, surprised. She laughed and went back to doing her crossword puzzle. "I don't think I do," I said sadly. "I feel pretty empty."

"I'm sure you've got one, too. Just close your eyes and imagine what it looks like," she said.

The prospects seemed confusing and exciting—a new place to explore, a new frontier, a new territory to map. That night at the hotel my secret garden appeared in a dream. I sat in a golden desert. Dunes rolled out like waves. Not a single plant grew. No trees. No flowers, no bees or birds. My heart felt arid and as dry as the parched land. If some divine essence thrived, somewhere inside me, it seemed buried beneath layers of sand. I awoke and strolled out into the hotel courtyard.

The pyramids loomed up the hill with the moon rising over the desert. This place knew the subtle power of dreams. The regal sphinx once stood nearly entirely covered with sand until Tuthmosis met the sun god in a dream and promised that if he would uncover it he would become pharaoh. He acted on his dream guidance and later reigned over Egypt. It's time for me to pay attention to dreams too, I thought. I walked to the top of the hill to the base of the Great Pyramid, and sand rolled on for miles. Out there somewhere in the distance grew a lush oasis, a secret garden in the desert.

At the end of the next day, after viewing Tutankhamen's gold mask, the scribe, and Pharaoh Akhenaten with the sun god in Cairo's Egyptian Museum, I asked the taxi driver to take me to the perfume shop. Julie worked on assignment while I set my own pace. From the outside, the boutique barely revealed its inner identity. Behind the stucco walls hid a refined, elegant showroom decorated with precious silk rugs, oriental carved wood, and mirrors behind rows of filigree hand-blown glass bottles. Light glimmered delicately across the gold-lined bottles of precious oils.

I handed Angelo's card to the dark-eyed man at the counter. "I'd like to meet Karim," I said.

"Wait here," he said.

In an instant, I felt a presence near my back and turned. A tall, elegant man extended his hand. "I'm Karim. Please step inside." He led me into a corner just out of view, to a thickly cushioned bench. "Sit, please. Will you have some hibiscus tea?"

Unaccustomed to such hospitality in a boutique, I stuttered. "Yyy … yes, please." He called out the order in Arabic to a teenaged kid. With my American, get-to-the-point mentality, I didn't want to waste time sitting down. I expected to try the perfumes and get on with the next task. But Karim (and the journey) imposed another rhythm. He puffed at a cigarette of black tobacco in a slow, even pace. He intended, it seemed, to create a bond and build trust before getting down to business. The teenager brought the red tea in a glass rimmed with gold. Karim wore a brown tailored shirt with short sleeves. His almond-shaped eyes glittered with an otherworldly light. From the small wrinkles at the corner of his mouth, I judged he must be about thirty-five. He handed me the tea, and I sat in uncomfortable silence until he breathed deeply and cleared his throat. "You live in France?"

I nodded. "I love it there."

"But you're American." He half-closed his eyes as if reading from an inner bulletin board. "You have no children and are going through a period of transition." I leaned back and crossed my arms. How did he know? The nose in Grasse must have told him, I thought. I uncrossed my arms and started to relax when I realized that I hadn't talked to the perfumer about children. My body stiffened. "You are uncomfortable?" Karim said.

"No, I'm fine," I lied, and he probably knew that too.

"You've had a year filled with loss and grief. Your heart's broken. On the outside your marriage looked fine, but inside you had no love."

Tears welled up in my eyes. "Stop," I wanted to say, but he continued. "I see this kind of reading is new to you. But you're one of us," he said.

Did he mean I could read from some inner book of people's lives, too? Karim continued. He knew about my worst childhood experiences, as if we had grown up together, and sensed the pain beneath my tough façade. I couldn't reason out how he knew. He spoke to the teenager, who arrived now with a tray of delicate hand-blown bottles and set them on the small table between us before disappearing behind a beaded curtain.

Karim seemed to sense my question, and he lifted the long stopper of a bottle and waved it in the warm air. A ceiling fan diffused the sweet, honeysuckle scent. "This is like your thoughts and feelings. They fill the air like this." He pointed to the invisible scent of flowers and spice that I could smell but not see. "You carry them in a cloud. All you need is a highly developed sense and to open doors of perception to sense it. But." He paused and looked at me intently. A little smile played at the corner of his mouth. "Most people are anosmic. You know what that means?"

I shook my head no and sipped the red tea; the sweet-tart taste of the hibiscus flower mixed with honey lit up my mouth with pleasure.

"They have no sense of smell. They do not have this sense of perception and since they do not experience it, they do not believe it exists. But you do." He let the words sink in. I do? I thought. I can't read people like that. "You are searching for something?" he continued.

Keep it businesslike and answer his question. "A perfume like Guerlain's Bagatelle would be nice. It's a floral scent. My favorite," I said. "*Bagatelle* in French means a trivial thing. A small thing," I said.

"But what you are searching for is not trivial. Come," he said and stood.

I hesitated, not knowing how far to trust him, but something whispered from my heart that it was okay. He took a key, opened a decorative iron gate, and stepped outdoors. A terrace garden with a fountain shaded by jasmine opened up like a small oasis. Papyrus grew and lotus flowers bloomed, sharing their sweet fragrance. The gurgling water mesmerized me as it flowed up from beneath the desert in a continual stream. Beautiful blue-tiled mosaics of the moon and stars decorated the walls.

"A secret garden!" I said. I felt fascinated by the synchronicity. "Is that aloe?"

"Yes, and hibiscus, Egyptian lupine." He pointed to the plants. "We have a long history of using plants to heal." The garden represents the paradise within, he explained. "You'll find yours, too, and be very happy. But you must find and plant a missing seed and cultivate it carefully."

"I'm not good at symbolic language," I said. "Say it straight."

"Your crises come from lack of self-love. Grow that seed of love and your world will blossom. That will heal your heart."

Yes, I wanted to say. I've yearned for love, the unconditional kind, for a long time and often mistaken lust and romance for love. But the unconditional kind held a divine mystery. I longed for it, imagined it, and yet didn't know how or where to find it. He said that it could be found and cultivated inside my secret garden of the soul.

"You are taking a trip up the Nile soon?" he said.

"Tomorrow."

"You have hard work to do. Your mind is making you very tired." He pointed to my head. "Why so much worry? It changes nothing." He held his huge dark eyes half-open like the Buddha's.

I shrugged.

"You have been looking in the wrong places," he said. "A mate and beautiful things will not bring real love and happiness. It's all inside."

He was right. I'd expected my husband to be *the* source of happiness, but the relationship turned dry and empty. The international business job had been an exciting challenge at first but also lost its appeal. I sighed, crossing my arms over my chest. Before leaving the Riviera, I'd been at a crossroads. Would I return to another executive job and continue climbing the corporate ladder or follow my soul's urge and do what I'd always dreamed of and write? The alternative, to forge a new way, seemed to have no maps or guides. It meant moving into unknown territory, befriending my intuition, and trusting that still, quiet inner voice of the soul for guidance. Turning toward that solitary and more difficult path seemed like an important but challenging and somewhat scary adventure.

We lingered in the silence a moment and then returned indoors. Karim presented the oils to me one by one. "I like sandalwood, red amber, and the Egyptian jasmine," I said.

He handed me one final bottle to try. "Sublime," I said, closing my eyes to take it in. Tears welled up. "I love it. What's it called?" More than a scent, it felt like a state of being. A top note of harmony. The heart note was one of peace. The base note felt like awareness as much as it could be captured in scent. It seemed so familiar and yet, like the perfume disappearing in the air, just out of grasp.

"It's called Ananda," he said. "Ananda means bliss."

"I love that one!" I said, and a subtle sensation of joy filled me.

He put the bottle back on the silver tray. "This is what you find deep in that sacred inner place. When you find it and carry it with you everywhere, then you'll know you've arrived at the destination." He pointed to my heart, and I felt in my cells, bones, and all of my being that he must be right. His teenaged assistant packaged the bottles, including a small bottle of Ananda, and took my money. Karim escorted me to the door and held out his hand. "If I can be of service..."

"Thanks," I said. "I'm grateful." But my emotions mixed between feeling grateful, awed, a little invaded, and also infatuated by the handsome stranger. He lifted his hand in a slight wave as I stepped across the threshold back into the setting Egyptian sun.

Later, staring out at the brown Nile waters from my cabin on the boat, the encounter played through my mind. Karim read hearts like others read books. He knew things about me that I could hardly admit to myself. He surely perceived my ugly thoughts along with the good ones. He could only do that through love, I decided. And it takes a lot of love to see someone unmasked and accept them. I longed for someone to love me like that. But first I needed to learn to love myself and give that love to others. Karim's unusual gift of clairvoyance added a new dimension to my explorations. He revealed a level of connection to humanity that both frightened and intrigued me.

The churning paddle wheel of the boat on the Nile and long hours on the water provided ample opportunity to take the seed of love Karim had offered and begin to plant it in my secret garden. I closed my eyes and imagined what the seed of love looked like. Small like a pomegranate tree seed, it held the power to grow into a strong tree that could bear a lot of fruit to share with others. The paddle wheel's hypnotic rhythm invited a deeper journey inside. Turning the focus inward, I slipped into a reverie. Inside, dunes appeared in my heart again, but beyond the dry sand I saw a gate and pushed it open.

An overgrown path led into an uncultivated, weedy place. Inside I found an empty reflecting pool, a deep well, and a temple in ruins. Some rosemary, thyme, and an untended rose bush grew by the well where a small patch of earth had once been cultivated as a healing herb garden. Here, I found a rusty spade and began to dig and dig, ripping out weeds and broken glass. The earth smelled rich, dark, and damp, almost sweet and full of potential. I took the tiny seed of love and planted it carefully underground and watered it with a bucket of fresh water from the deep well. In my mind's eye, I marked the spot with a stick and now needed patience.

With the smallest amount of water, a desert comes to life in a quick, furious frenzy. I scheduled regular moments to go inside and tend this inner garden during the trip. The work consisted of regular periods of meditation, self-inquiry, and reflection on grief and loss. In the silence, a tiny seed of love and another of peace sprouted and took root. During the day, when I ventured out onto the boat's deck with a few pas-sengers or traveled out to the crocodile temple and bartered with merchants, I'd think of the love growing in my heart and bring that into my words and actions.

During the next scheduled rendezvous with my secret garden, I imagined what the tree of love would look like in full bloom and how my garden would appear after a year or two of care. Wise gardeners anticipate what their gardens will look like decades into the future. In my future landscape, a cascade flowed clear and pure. A still reflecting pool filled with koi mirrored the azure sky. Tiny orchids; huge, multi-colored camellias; and magnolia flowers blossomed. Cherry blossoms drifted on the breeze and decorated the path. I saw landscapes, including rocks and mountains, seas and plains. The walls had fallen, and I invited people to take healing herbs and consume the fruits from the large tree that looked like pomegranates. My garden contained its own unique template for perfection. I simply needed to grow into it. By fertilizing and cultivating the inner landscape, I sensed, this would also create a serene environment around me, where the inner and outer would eventually converge, one reflecting the other, and bring wholeness to heal this empty, broken heart.

Visualizing Your Secret Garden

Everyone, I believe, has a secret garden. Most of us don't realize it until we imagine it. Using guided visualization activates the imagination and opens up the dialogue with your psyche, your soul-Self. It's a form of dreaming while awake. The soul communicates using a subtle language of images and scenes and often reveals surprising and delightful things. To anchor subtle impressions from the psyche or imagination, they need to be captured or materialized in writing and images. To begin this experience, prepare a notebook and pen or a recording device to record your impressions once you finish. It's ideal to keep a box of crayons, colored pencils, or collage materials at hand, too. You may want to have a friend read the following visualization to you or record it in your own voice and play it as you sit back and relax.

Find a comfortable, quiet place where you'll not be disturbed for about twenty minutes. This will be a time to relax and attend only to yourself. Begin with some relaxing breaths. Breathe in love and light, and when you breathe out, let go of all of the tensions, anxieties, and concerns of the day. Breathe in again and let go of the tension in your jaws, shoulders, hips, and anywhere else. As you exhale, allow the tension to release.

Close your eyes and imagine walking down a cobblestone street. Feel the uneven stones underfoot. The sun's rays warm your shoulders, and a gentle breeze caresses your face. In the distance a gurgling creek runs through a field, and a wooden bridge arches over it. Cross over the bridge and continue to follow the path. Up ahead you see a gate. This is the entrance to your secret garden. Find the key in your pocket and open the gate. Cross over the threshold. As you enter into your sacred space, notice the colors, the smells, and the spaces around you. Is it light? Do you notice the plants? Do you see any buildings or people?

Continue walking and move toward the center of your secret garden. It may contain a fountain, a waterfall, a pool, or something else. Explore some more until you find the most sacred place. Is it a temple, a protected house, or a grove of ancient trees? Make an offering of gratitude to your garden for receiving you. The gift you give may be a word of thanks, a flower, or something you value. Open your hands and heart and in return receive whatever messages or objects may be given to you to help you in your explorations. Feel the peace and the silence in this inner place. Linger here for a moment and enjoy your secret garden.

When you're ready, take with you what you need. Return to the threshold of your sacred space. Notice any last details that attract your attention. Pay attention to how your body, mind, and spirit feel as you linger here. When you arrive at the gate, take one last look around, then step out and close it. Remember that you can return whenever you like. Walk gently down the path. Return back over the arched bridge that goes over the creek, back down to the cobblestone street, and back to where you initially left from. When you're ready, open your eyes.

Take a moment to record what you experienced. Describe what you saw, how you felt, and who, if anyone, you met. Did you receive a gift or a message? Capture the feelings in writing or use a recording device and speak into it. To cultivate the language of symbols more deeply, you may want to draw, paint, or make a collage of your secret garden. Search the Internet to come up with specific images if you have them in mind. Let the scene take shape naturally as you work with it. Once you finish, you may want to keep the image in a place where you will see it often.

Synchronicity and Paying Attention to Signs

When you commit to a spiritual journey like exploring your inner secret garden of the soul, very often the world around will conspire to help. Events may arise. People you think of may appear unexpectedly. Someone says exactly what you need to hear or you may see a scene or images during the day that recall a dream you had the night before. These magical synchronicities bring messages and signs that the universe is dancing with us. Encounters with the perfumer and Karim arrived in my life at a moment of serious soul-searching about what directions to take and lit the way with clues of what was to come. As you set out on this mystical adventure to discover the deeper places of your soul, pay attention to the synchronicities and signs along your path. You may want to keep a notebook as a way to keep track of your synchronistic experiences.

There is only one journey. Going inside yourself.
—RAINER MARIA RILKE

Chapter 2
When a Rose
Is More Than a Rose:
Learning the Soul's Language

Crossing from the ordinary world of business life into the secret garden invited in big changes. And change is scary. It brings death of old ways and the birth of something new but not yet known. On the return home from Egypt to the South of France, death and rebirth shook my foundations. While on the trip down the Nile, I celebrated the shift in circumstances from international business executive to spiritual seeker with a ceremony. Like a graduation ceremony, a wedding, or a funeral, a ritual marks a significant shift in one's condition. It acknowledges in a real, conscious way the change in life circumstances and celebrates or grieves it. Doing a ritual to let go of old ways seemed appropriate and natural.

While oxen tilled the hard soil along the Nile banks and women washed clothes in the murky waters with the backdrop of scorched hills, the churning paddle wheel of the boat pushed me toward the city of Luxor. Even before the trip to Egypt I'd decided not to return to the corporate world. I aimed to write—something I'd felt called to do since childhood. In my cabin on the boat, I imagined all of the accouterments of the business role I'd just let go of piled at my feet: briefcases; suits; calculators; the daily, weekly, monthly, quarterly annual reports; and job evaluations.

I stood by the round window and in a sweeping movement extended my hands from head to toe to remove all of these things from my being. I gathered them in an imaginary stack and tossed them out the porthole. In my mind's eye, they fell out the window and slid deep into the wide, murky river. As we chugged forward with each new turn of the paddle wheel, the business stuff stayed far behind and sank deeper into the water. This ritual act of liberation brought on a dizzying sense of lightness, excitement, and relief combined with the dread of losing a role that had been vital to my identity.

Back home in Antibes, France, a week later, a dream welled up from the heart of my secret garden.

I am back on the boat, chugging along the Nile tugging at a thick rope. At the end of it, through the murky water, a businesswoman hangs limp. I frantically pull and yank to drag her back to the surface. "Help me," I plead with the wise captain. "I've got to revive her. Please help me." He stands on deck, arms crossed placidly, and watches my panicked struggle. He shakes his head "no" slowly back and forth. "Let her go," he says, looking down at me. "She's dead."

I shot up in bed and found myself trembling and sweating. Someone died! What a tragic dream. And I could do nothing to save that poor woman, I thought. But with a little reflection I saw that the dead woman was the part of me I'd dumped overboard with all of the business accessories in Egypt. Her death had left a vacuum just as real as the death of a friend or family member.

Part of me desired to return to the comfortable but painful path of a creatively stymied businesswoman rather than grow into my new role as writer and seeker. As a business executive, I knew the ropes, how to function, how to make money, how to climb the corporate ladder. That old way felt familiar, but would not lead to happiness. The new path into the secret garden required learning new rules and new approaches. It meant listening to and interpreting dreams that began to rise up from deep places in my soul.

But wouldn't it be so much easier to return to the old, familiar ways? I could try it again, for a little while at least, I thought. Doubts crept in, fostered by people around me. My parents wondered why I had invited such a drastic change from lucrative business career to seeker and writer. Most of my friends who had envied my job with all the international travel did, too. Was I crazy? Had I made the right decision?

Still near the beginning of the point where the paths diverged, it would not be too difficult to cut back and rejoin the old, predictable path, get another corporate job, and fall into familiar, numb ways. But those old ways were driving me to another kind of death: the death of my soul. My inner life looked like a desert, but I yearned for a lush, tropical garden. Amid the doubts and questions about returning to the business world or forging ahead in a new direction, another dream revealed a new piece of the puzzle.

A plane crashes in the Mediterranean in front of my apartment. The fuselage breaks into three parts. I dive into the sea to rescue survivors. On the sea floor, a woman in a business suit lies dead. Nothing can bring her back to life. But a baby sits nearby. I'm overjoyed to see the baby and scoop it into my arms. It peers into me with wide, dark eyes so profound and beautiful that I know I am peering into my own soul. A sense of awe and profound love overwhelm me. I clench the infant tightly to my chest and swim hard to bring her up. I need to save her, to carry her to the surface where she will grow up and thrive.

I jerked awake in shock from the crash. The dream played into my worst fears of falling and dying in a plane crash. My grief at the death of the businesswoman mingled with electrifying joy and awe at retrieving a beautiful, healthy baby. The newborn spiritual child awakened an inexplicable sense of purity, beauty, and mystery, not unlike feelings connected with watching a splendid sunrise or seeing a brilliant butterfly alight on a perfect rose. But the feeling ran deeper and held a strong yearning to protect. I experienced deep maternal love and affection.

The renowned Swiss analyst Carl Jung referred to the dream baby as the soul-Self, the spiritual part of us that yearns to be born and find expression. The work of nurturing the newborn would require no less commitment and attention than caring for a physical baby. In some ways I sensed it would demand more. It would mean eliminating old habits and energy-draining behaviors so the baby would receive the best nourishment. The infant soul would need to become my focus in every instant. In every action and thought, I would have to consider her needs above all. I'd acquired a new charge, a newborn baby, and like a physical child, my child (an aspect of my soul-Self) guided the way through her chidings, whimpering, and smiles. I wanted nothing more than to please her and make her happy. This became my new goal.

But how do you care for a metaphysical child? No operating manual or instructions came with it, and this was not something taught in school. I thought of friends with a newborn. Their whole lives shifted focus from parties and pleasures to how they could satisfy their child. They stopped drinking. They stopped going out. The rooms of their house transformed with protective barriers, a special nursery room, diapers, toys. They learned to live to the rhythm of their baby and make sacrifices of sleep and personal desires for the baby's comfort. They could not socialize much, but they didn't seem to mind. Their joy came from caring for their child and watching him or her grow. I sensed that my new baby required some of the same life changes.

Elsie, a dream expert, worked at the bookstore. Maybe her experiences would help me work with dreams. I called her up to ask. "Yes, pay attention to your dreams," she said. "At their best they provide hints about your inner life. A lot of good information will come to you this way. They're your soul speaking to you." I waited impatiently, silently on the other end of the receiver. But she said no more. I bit my lip.

"I don't understand. Can't you tell me what it means?" I begged. I'd described my recent dreams to her. "Something strange is happening. It's like a dialogue has opened up between my inner, dream world and my waking, conscious one."

"Yes," she said, reflecting. "That will happen when you turn the focus inside toward your spirit."

"But how am I supposed to know what these things mean? What am I supposed to do with all of this information?" My hands shook with excitement.

"You hold the keys with the answers," she said softly. "Most people are fragmented, cut off from what they really feel, from their soul-Self."

I sighed deeply. "I don't get it."

"Think of it like defragmenting a computer. The human mind is separated into compartments—the conscious, the subconscious, and higher consciousness. We're familiar with our conscious mind because we use it when we're awake. The information in other parts is spread out in bits, and dreaming is a creative process that helps piece them together."

"So you've done this too?"

"Yes, but it's different for everybody," she said. "It's also a very exciting adventure, and tools like dreams and meditation will help grow your soul and open the doors between the different levels of mind."

"If you can see so much, can you tell me, did I make the right decision in leaving business?" I asked. I felt ready to surrender all of my decision making to her for guidance. Please, just tell me what to do, I thought.

She laughed. "After those dreams, your answer seems pretty clear. Don't you think?" she said.

"I feel better mostly. And in some ways worse. It seems they're saying I'm on the right track and to keep going. Let the businesswoman die and trust this new path. But it's uncomfortable and unknown territory."

"Don't confuse security and comfort with peace. You have the answers and it works like this," she said. "You listen from deep inside, then act on what feels right. If you make a wrong decision, you'll know soon enough and you can change direction." Then I described to her some of the garden dreams. "Pay attention to your wise inner gardener," she said.

"My inner gardener?"

"Yes. She's the part of you that points out the junk and leads the way. She represents the higher, wiser part of yourself who knows what to cultivate and how. She knows that a rose can be more than just a rose."

"How's that?" I said.

"A rose on the street may be just a flower. But if a man plucks it and brings it to you, then it takes on deeper meaning. It might represent budding passion, for example."

"My inner gardener speaks the language of symbols even if I don't?"

"You got it," she said.

We said goodbye and I hung up with more questions than answers. This must be crazy, I thought. No one pays attention to dreams except ancient Egyptians and biblical characters. Then I recalled the power in the love I felt for my baby as I clenched her in my arms and vowed never to let her go. It all came through a dream!

Paying attention to dreams and emotions taught me to trust my wisdom heart. The word *emotion* comes from a Latin word that means "to move one forward." If a situation felt wrong, like the idea of going back into the corporate world, then my emotions nudged me to move in a new direction. But it is not enough to rely only on a sense of ease for decision making. Some actions push us beyond our comfort zone. That means we're growing beyond our usual boundaries and self-imposed limitations. It feels intimidating and scary, yet very right. The challenge becomes facing the fear and getting on with the right action. More than a question of moving toward what felt good, decisions required relying on what felt right. Perhaps if I found my inner gardener and learned to listen, she would help guide the way.

Secret Garden Meditation

A secret garden needs time and space to grow. There's no miracle about the gardens that grow best; they receive regular attention. You may want to schedule a daily time and place to sit quietly and explore your inner sacred space of the spirit. Find a quiet spot perhaps in a garden, at a sacred place in your home, or in nature. Pick a time when you can easily shut out the world and enter inside. Don't allow phones, Internet, or people to disturb your special time to cultivate your inner secret garden of the soul. Shift your focus inside and let go of the world's demands.

Say a mantra or a prayer of protection or imagine yourself filled with pure, white light. If you have difficulty sitting quietly, try focusing on the light of a candle for a few minutes. Imagine its warmth filling your heart. Watch your breath and breathe easily without blocking or controlling it. Sit for a minute, then build up to five minutes. If you keep up the practice, you'll naturally increase the amount of time. This act of making time for your sacred Self is an ancient discipline that will bring great benefits. It allows a space for solutions to problems to arise and improves concentration, and your sense of serenity will grow. It also stimulates dream life.

Listening to Dreams for Guidance

Working with dreams and symbols is a way to establish a dialogue with your soul. Many people say, "I don't dream." But we all dream approximately thirty minutes out of every ninety-minute sleep cycle. To work with dreams it's ideal to keep a notepad, pen, and night light by the bed. Some people prefer a recording device. Before going to bed, make a suggestion to yourself: "I will recall my dreams." Repeat it and make efforts to recall them. A suggestion can be made to request help on a particular question or problem as well. In the morning, try to wake up naturally without an alarm.

Immediately on waking, remain still and reflect on the last images in your mind. If you can't recall images, then write down a feeling, a word, a song, a color, or anything that comes to mind from that deeper place. It's ideal to record dreams in present tense and give them titles. Writing in present tense will bring you immediately back into the dream when you return later to review it. Giving titles will help you to better summarize what they mean.

The language of dreams is symbols. Symbols are the language of the soul and they point to deeper meanings. Imbued with emotional power, they are like nuggets of gold in the secret garden. When we're cut off from them, we remove ourselves from a vital, creative source of wisdom and insight. When connected to them, we can use them to find solutions to problems and understand ourselves in a profound way.

Learning the language of symbols requires effort and practice. Interpreting the images that appear in dreams and daily life becomes a uniquely individual experience. For example, a house often represents shelter or the place where the soul resides, but if you're an architect it may be a work-related symbol. We benefit by learning our personal symbols, and this takes patience and practice by meditating on the symbols. As symbols like the secret garden grow through periods of blossoming and change, they may reflect an inner state, reveal deeper feelings, and help weave together the fragmented pieces of the Self. My garden has appeared as a desert, as an oasis filled with huge flowers, as an island paradise, and in many different seasons representing where I'm at emotionally and spiritually.

If you'd like to explore dream work, before going to bed at night review your dreams. Consider what the symbols might mean for you. You may want to use symbol dictionaries for a history of the images; however, your dreams are very personal and dream dictionaries that give specific definitions for images like a black cat or a scarab usually fall short of what they actually mean to you. Consider instead what qualities or properties the images, animals, or people in your dreams contain. If you dream of a bear, what do you associate with it? Teddy bears may be huggable and represent something to hold on to for security. Bears in the wild can be both protective of their young and very fierce. They also hibernate. If you dream of a person, think of what you associate with them: Success? Insecurity? Artistic abilities? When they appear in your dreams, they may represent these aspects of yourself.

There is not a moment when I do not feel the presence of a Witness whose eye misses nothing and with whom I strive to keep in tune.

—MAHATMA GANDHI

Chapter 3

Meeting the Inner Gardener

When entering into sacred inner space like the secret garden, we're never alone, even though sometimes it may feel that way. There's a constant, if invisible, presence that guides and prompts, and the journey becomes about learning to sense and trust it. Conscious awareness of that presence represents awakening to the Divine. Elsie, the dream expert, called it the "inner gardener." That presence is not separate or outside, but in the beginning it may appear so wise and enlightened that it becomes difficult to believe that it is a real and truer aspect of our being. As the inner gardener, the soul-Self, began to speak with me, I struggled to follow her guidance.

In Antibes, as I settled into the artist's and spiritual seeker's life, loneliness invaded the long days at my desk. I yearned for companionship and especially to share this new path with a mate. When Kalin, a race-car driver with an impressive Lamborghini and stylish clothes, showed up at the table next to mine at a Cap d'Antibes beach café and invited me to dinner, I felt someone had answered my prayers. But my inner gardener said, "Be careful." We'd just met, too, my inner gardener and I. Not unlike cartoons where a devil stood on one shoulder urging me to indulge in his self-indulgent fantasies and an angel stood on the other encouraging good actions, my inner gardener stood with me like a good angel whispering the right direction to take. "Be wary of that man," she said. "Take it slow." Her voice echoed up through dreams, in quiet walks, in observations about his gait.

At Antibes' port, where multi-million-dollar yachts docked, Kalin and I walked and chatted while admiring ships with teak decks and brass fittings named "Great Expectations," "Bravado," and "My Best Friend." The inner gardener warned me to pay attention to details and keep my distance from the smooth racer. In a dream, this man appeared as a bear. Bears can be playful, but they also tear things apart. But dreams can take time to trust and understand. Was the bear really him? (It certainly felt like it.) Or was it someone else? Was this a game? Did a threat really exist or was I making it up?

On the stroll, I noticed Kalin's walk. His body seemed twisted. He could not walk straight, but instead he walked crooked, in a sort of zigzag. No physical illness or accident accounted for this. A flash, like a news bulletin in Times Square, ran through my mind. "This man is crooked," it said. Though I didn't understand how, every cell of my being knew it was true. My wise gardener made herself known through that ripple of intuition. She wanted to protect me from danger. A chill of shock ran up my spine. I excused myself and went home in tears with no explanation and no intention of seeing him again.

The next morning he sent a bouquet of fragrant white lilies nearly as large as my mahogany table and wooed me to dine at La Colombe d'Or, an exclusive restaurant outside the old fortified walls of St. Paul de Vence, where Matisse, Picasso, and other famous artists once traded paintings and sculpture for room and board. Some of their paintings still decorate the walls. By then I'd begun to doubt my flashes of intuition about Kalin. He wasn't really crooked, was he? It was just my imagination, wasn't it? Just look at the lovely flowers. They must be a sign of some sensitivity and goodness, right?

My desire for companionship battled with my intuition. I brushed aside the feelings of the day before until they lay buried beneath my consciousness. After an amiable lunch on the terrace with rosé wine, I convinced myself that my wise inner gardener had made a mistake. My intuition was wrong. Kalin wasn't a bad guy really. He seemed generous, attentive, and in hot pursuit. My wise gardener sat beside me, arms crossed, and sighed.

"He appears to be fine," I reasoned her away and stuck to outer appearances.

"Okay, do it your way," she said and disappeared.

Some weeks later, Kalin called. "I've got to catch a flight, but I lost my wallet. It will take some time to get the credit cards renewed. Can you lend a hand?" He stayed at one of the expensive hotels on the Cap d'Antibes. It matched his persona and the expensive car. The hotel wouldn't accept checks, but would I accept his check and put the hotel bill on my credit card? I agreed to pay his bill in exchange for his check. He returned to London for a few days with promises to return. When I called the number on his card, his phone service was disconnected. His friends reassured me that all was well; he'd been in touch and would be back soon. I waited impatiently for a call.

It came from my banker, who called and announced that his check had bounced. Kalin returned, apologized, and promised he would pay back the sum. I knew by then that my wise gardener was right, and the money had vanished into the void of his lavish lifestyle. In addition, a mysterious anonymous person called to say that Kalin owned nothing and was a certified thief. Perhaps anybody else would have suspected his ruse, but my foolish side wanted to believe in the appearance and charm, wanted to believe that he liked me, that he might be the right mate.

Then a policeman called; Kalin was in jail. He had stolen the Lamborghini sports car; his credit cards were frauds; he had even faked his passport and used a false name. A con artist, a total imposter, had played on my desires for the Cinderella dream and companionship and won a Monopoly trip to jail. I had hoped for uprightness, integrity, and potentially a relationship. Longing overshadowed the voice of conscience.

What a blow to my ego and emotions. My wise gardener had tried to warn me. "Appearances deceive," she said. "Look deeper." But my desires had canceled out her voice, and I paid the price. My shame at having made such a stupid mistake against her guidance sent me plunging into remorse. I withdrew into the secret garden to atone for my error. Atone, at-one. This period represented the effort of becoming *at one* with my soul-Self, of merging my inner guidance from my wise gardener with my actions, and fully trusting this deeper voice even when my rational mind tried to convince me that all things on the surface appeared fine. Later, once my pain and anger subsided, I thanked Kalin for being the teacher who showed me the importance of listening to her.

The inner gardener protects me and leads me to higher ground—*when I listen*. Going against her loving guidance causes pain and hurtful repercussions. Throughout my adventures, she watched and protected. Sometimes she appeared in dreams and warned me of things to come; sometimes she made herself known in the still, silent voice of conscience; and sometimes her words arrived in the form of a friend or stranger who would unwittingly say exactly the message that resonated with the inner work taking shape at that moment. Once on a mountain path, she stopped me with a gentle but firm hand. My next step would have fallen on a poisonous viper. I didn't know the decision to follow her unconditionally would mark the discovery of a new world of powerful intuition unfolding in my secret garden.

More About the Wise Gardener

This awakening to inner guidance took me by surprise. My inner gardener had just proved that she knew better than I did about what was good for me. Though I was just getting to know her, she seemed to protect me like a mother, advise me like a best friend, and watch over me like an angel. I sensed her presence listening and participating in my days as I walked the cobblestone streets across the Place Nationale in Antibes or up the Chemin de la Croix toward the chapel and lighthouse on the Cap. She was a shape shifter too. In a dream she showed up as a luminous being of light, as a wise mother, and as a business mentor. The peace and strength she emanated soothed me and I trusted her guidance beyond all else.

It's hard to explain this relationship as it grew. I'd not ever put credence in guides or thought of protective forces before. But I saw in her a glowing presence of light and tender compassion. She could not harm. She is the elevated, better part of me and we are not separate, but in dreams and visions she appeared as a separate person because I was incapable of imagining that I held the peace and light that shined forth from her. It took time to gain the confidence that within me and within each of us burns a spark of the Divine. Filled with light, she rarely spoke words, but emanated a wisdom and understanding beyond any that I consciously knew. As time has passed, we have merged in desires and aims.

At first, getting to know this deeper soul-Self may seem at odds with all we're taught. Though we're often outward directed, driven to impress and convince others of our worth through work, social relationships, and possessions, the wise gardener holds different values. She cares less about the material displays and appearances but sees into the heart of the matter and hears the whispers of our deepest desires and motives that lie hidden beneath the appearances we paint. She reminds us of who we are even when we have convinced ourselves that we are the mask. She is the deeper soul-Self who lives in a world driven by ideals of the spirit.

She became my teacher. As I put more trust in her, she revealed things that I needed to eliminate in order to grow, and she led me to the right experiences that would help me to expand. Through dreams, she encouraged me when I made improvements and chided me when I fell. She warned and protected me from difficulties. She also introduced me to other aspects of myself that lived in doubt and fear, and insisted that I get my house in order. None of this work was easy or quick. It took many hours of introspection to comprehend, long days of applying what I'd learned, and months and years of practice to change.

But the wise gardener guides the way to the right answers. The greatest pain and suffering comes from hearing her voice and ignoring it. We each know her presence. She is the most intimate, divine part of us. She is the still, small voice whispering from within the spirit. "Expand your heart," she urges. "Grow, grow." She shares a secret, that we are not separate, but when I let go of having things my way we become one. When I accepted her gentle ways she gave me so much inner work that it became a full-time job.

Befriending Your Wise Gardener

The greatest pain and suffering we create for ourselves comes from hearing the voice of our inner gardener, the voice of our conscience, and ignoring her guidance. We each know her presence. She is the most intimate, divine part of us. But many of us have been out of touch with her for a long time. It may help to attune to your wise gardener through visualization. Begin with a protective prayer or call in light to surround you on this inward journey. Take some time now to sit quietly and enter into the heart of your secret garden; invite your wise gardener to join you.

As she comes into view, you move closer to her to get to know her better. (For some of you, this guide may be a masculine figure.) In your way, approach your inner gardener and learn more about how you can work together. Will you embrace her? Will you have a dialogue that you might write out? Will you sit in silence and learn to trust her? Before you leave your garden, reflect on how you might continue to develop this relationship. Ask her for advice if you will. You may want to make a collage, draw an image of her, or find a photo that resembles your imagination of how she appears.

Through listening, practice, and observation, you will become aware of the subtle differences between the chattering mind full of wants and the still, small voice of your inner gardener. The mind screams that its needs be met. The inner gardener speaks in whispers with few words. The mind can act as an instrument of arrogance, while the soul, or wise gardener, functions based on humility. With this in mind, do your actions and choices reflect the mind's attitude or the soul's?

Trusting Intuition

Messages from your soul, your inner gardener, arrive in subtle, barely perceptible flashes. Everyone receives intuitive information, which helps guide and protect us. The ways we receive intuitive insights are unique to each individual. Some people hear words with their inner, subtle hearing. Others see pictures or scenes. Some people feel energies and sense if something is beneficial or not.

You can develop your intuition by paying attention to how the information arrives for you. A good way to do this is to keep an intuition journal and note your hunches and experiences. Does the information arrive in images, through sound, in a distinct feeling? Keep track of how the intuitive hits play out. This will help you to refine and better interpret the information you receive. The more you act on the subtle messages, the more your intuition will grow. Recording your experiences will help you to learn to trust this wise source of information and deepen your relationship with your inner gardener.

Body and mind, and spirit, all combine to make the creature,
human and divine.

—ELLA WHEELER WILCOX

Chapter 4

Breaking New Ground: Tending Inner Life in the Secret Garden

The inner gardener inspires commitment to change. She knows that the little steps will make a huge difference in future harvests, and she encourages us to take them. Those steps might seem difficult at first, but the payoff of growing a healthy and thriving inner life is worth it. She encourages timeouts to listen to emotions and conscience. "Reflect on life's experiences," she whispers. "And learn from them. Drop whatever makes the journey heavy."

Getting involved in spiritual pursuits can become passionately consuming, and I yearned to spend whole days in meditation and working with dreams. But paying for the apartment, food, clothes, and other necessities while not earning a regular salary required keeping my feet on the ground, maintaining a budget, and assessing what I truly needed. The Riviera, more than most any other place on Earth, appeals to the senses and thrives on desires. The azure sea hangs next to the rocky coast dotted with parasoled private beaches; ships with helicopter pads adorn the ports; shops of silver sandals, pink leather bags, and 18-karat gold-set jewels glimmer in the hot sun; and the markets serve up thousands of opportunities to revel in sensory delights.

The world's wealthiest and most famous celebrities buy houses on the capes or escape taxes in Monaco. Gold Rolexes and Rolls-Royces are almost as common as Timex watches and Fords. The air at Antibes' covered market reeks of *herbes de Provence* and roses from the Cap d'Antibes' last greenhouses. Back-country farmers sell eggs "from happy chickens," smelly goat cheeses, Corsican sausages, and rows and rows of olives spiced with chilies and thyme. With the multitude of temptations, a constant yearning for something always gnawed at me. A luscious Ott rosé wine, sumptuous black cherries, melons, Arabica coffee, and dark, dark chocolate. The desires seemed to run on endlessly. This yearning afflicted tourists, too. Their envious eyes turned toward the yacht owners sunbathing on slick decks or stared hungrily at clients eating behind the windows at Les Vieux Murs.

Why not transcend the yearnings? What would it feel like to no longer feel consumed with desires? How would I react without my usual three cups of Ethiopian Arabica espresso and dark chocolate–filled croissants? Prompted by my inner gardener, I decided on an experiment. For one day I would fast and drink only water for twenty-four hours. I'd not ever gone without a meal in my life. This would test my resolve and offer a new way to relate to the world, one where I would not be a consumer.

My stomach growled and my mind grumbled at the idea, but deeper feelings of exhilaration lifted me above the uneven cobblestones as I headed toward the port by the city walls that Sunday. The sun rose clear and warm, turning the water pink and gold, until it lifted itself fully out of the sea and into the air. Hot and bright, it beat down with the light loved by Picasso, who had lived in one of the town's towers (now a museum). The market bustled with tourists and locals out for choice pieces of fish—*dorade, loup*, rock fish, sole from the North— and fruits heavy with sugar: sweet Cavaillon melons, shiny blood-red cherries from the Var, tiny wild strawberries.

Their fragrances wafted through me. I observed the scents enter my nostrils and my senses explode with pleasure. My eyes drank in their vibrant shades of red and orange, but I resisted consuming them. Odd, I thought. I've looked at most things with an intention to possess, use, or consume. How unusual to see those beautiful fruits in their splendor and not act on desire. My tummy grumbled some more, but my resolve held fast. My mind attached to things, but I stood back as the witness.

The walk through the other market aisles past my favorite chocolates, blood oranges, and eggplants left me in awe at the blackness of the dark chocolate, the aroma of the oranges, and the purplish color of the vegetables. My mind yearned for them. "I have got to have those," it insisted. But a sense of surprise overcame me. I had the power to act or not. When my mind went out to grasp objects, if I settled in like the witness and watched its yearning, it had no power over me. Instead my mind became an instrument, and I, the witness, took control when I remained alert and aware. This realization released me from bondage to material desires.

I walked down the side street to the square—past the colorful dresses, the exotic jewelry shop with Thai prints and carvings, in front of the handcrafted Moustiers dishes, past the fresh pasta store where the sublime tomato-basil sauce cost as much as the handmade pasta—and the same experience recurred. I admired the colorful woven clothes and butterfly pasta, appreciated the work that went into their creation, felt inspired by their forms, and that sufficed. For one day, the heavy chains of consumerism and desire fell away. I refused to allow my senses to enslave me.

A sense of lightness and elation accompanied this new direction on the path of discovery. I usually swam through the sea of life caught up in the madness and the rush, unable to watch my inner workings. But for once I stepped out onto the riverbanks to simply observe the currents of thought flow past. I observed my body feeling hungry; my mind said it felt hungry too and wandered around from color to scent to texture, demanding it be fed. United with my inner gardener, I felt happily detached from it all. This game revealed a delightful discovery: to simply be, without goals or aims of acquiring and consuming, liberates me, if only temporarily. It gives me the choice to control the senses and mind and not to let them control me.

Stepping out of the river of consumerism to stand on the bank as an observer liberated me for a lifetime. It turned me from a slave to desires into a free woman. The exquisite Italian leather handbags at the San Remo market no longer held power over me. Nor did the sweet-scented soaps and oils in the boutiques. That one experience remains with me even today as I walk through markets and malls. This doesn't mean I no longer consume. I do. It means I decide consciously what to buy.

Veering into excesses even in the spiritual realm, such as too much asceticism and fasting, can cause harm. Instead I aimed to maintain a healthy balance and set out to fast one day a week. The next day I returned to luscious croissants for breakfast along with rich espresso. The yearning to possess certain things remained—a golden Tahitian pearl, a teak table for the terrace, a crystal vase, good wine. But I returned inside the garden of the mind and reflected before buying and consuming. Money equaled a certain amount of time and energy. Was I willing to exchange it for a watch or a new car? Did I really need these things? I did not realize at the time that a longer fast to test my will would be in store and all of the beautiful things I'd collected and acquired over a decade would soon disappear. The sea-view apartment would be left behind like the fragments of a dream. The one thing certain about life is that it promises constant change. Nothing ever remains the same.

Tend the Secret Garden or Shop?

I ultimately made a decision to examine my lifestyle. How much of a sacrifice did I intend to make for things, and how much time did I want to invest in my secret garden? Each day I considered what I consumed and what I thought I needed. Like a witness, I observed how my mind demanded a glass of Minuty white wine with dinner, how I perpetually kept a bottle of champagne *au frais* and used expensive perfumed soaps and sumptuous Guerlain fragrances. I *needed* a regular trip to the coiffeur and massages. I *had* to wear fashionable Kenzo T-shirts and designer jeans and absolutely could not give up the regular trips to the Thermes, the sea water spa at the Hermitage on the cliff in Monaco. I had acquired South-of-France habits that demanded fulfillment for a sense of happiness. And they demanded that I work more to make more money and support this lifestyle.

Shopping and consuming had enslaved me as the businesswoman. Caught up in the game of acquiring something new, better, bigger, and more fashionable, Debra, the executive, became bound to credit cards, to working more, and to a way of life that kept her out of the secret garden and distant from her wise gardener. By living in debt to material things, she could not easily make the choice to change jobs or devote time to creative aspirations. Rather than think for herself, corporate Debra allowed the media to greatly influence her choices and play on her insecurities about aging, fitting in, and owning the socially acceptable things.

But objects like a new phone or TV quickly lose their sheen and go out of fashion, while she would be left with the bills. Possessing things required time, energy, and sacrifice. As a businesswoman I had made the calculations of how much something cost, but didn't add in the amount of time, energy, and worry it cost over the long term. I didn't stop to think that the money I exchanged for an antique mahogany ship chest or another pair of designer shoes equaled precious time and energy. Nor did I consider others who might be in need, or of ways to use money that could be of service.

This new Debra wasn't meant to be an ascetic or take vows of poverty. But I knew that if I wanted to devote time to cultivating the secret garden and write, I needed to pare down, clean out closets, let go of waste, and eliminate costly desires that left me a slave to credit cards and a corporate job. The decision marked a step in reassessing what really matters. At about the same time I became friends with Monsieur Ponts, an old French man, very *vieille France*, very traditional. We lived on the same block and met on our daily walks. As his health declined and he could no longer walk, I carried baguettes to his apartment and observed the slow deterioration of old age and his loss of independence.

"Take those pictures out of my drawer," he said one afternoon, pointing with a gnarled finger to his credenza. He showed me photos of him with his lovely wife in their healthy, wealthy thirties; photos of his expensive car; photos with an entourage of important people; photos in a uniform; photos of his beautiful villa filled with expensive antiques. "They're all gone," he said. "Every last thing." A certain sad, bittersweetness filled his sigh. "We think it will always be the same. But in the end you can't hold on to anything." His melancholy and a realization of the ephemeral nature of my own physical body made me want to cry—and to find something enduring that would not fade. This motivated me to dig deeper in the realm of the secret garden and tighten my bond to the higher self, my wise, inner gardener. She held the secrets to what endured and pointed the way to the eternal and unchanging Divine.

Weeding Out Obstacles

The more time we invest in gaining things, the less time we can spend exploring the inner landscape. It's a trade-off. What costly desires keep you out of your inner garden? Are you ready to let go of any of these? How can you simplify your life? Limiting desires is a spiritual practice that not only helps us to gain perspective about what's really important; it also makes a considerable contribution to a better environment for the earth. When we buy less, we also use fewer resources.

Cultivating the Garden of the Mind

If you imagine your mind as a garden with all of your thoughts and feelings growing inside, what does it look like? What kind of fruits and flowers will it give you? We spend many hours concerned with outer appearance. But the inner garden of the mind creates the conditions where we can thrive. When we become conscious of the mental chatter and its desires, we can consciously choose what we want in our lives. Conscious action means freedom from impulse. It also means we create an inner terrain that can flourish into a beautiful life.

The mind interprets the data from the senses and acts as the intermediary between the outer and inner worlds, but it needs direction. From within the secret garden, you can watch its workings and guide it in the direction that coincides with your higher aims. Take a moment to step back inside your sacred space and begin to observe the mind. Watch its chatter, its demands and its desires. You can guide it by defining soulful values that point it in the direction you wish to travel on your life journey. Cultivate it as you would a sacred garden and plant in it only desires and thoughts that you wish to see grow into beautiful flowers.

Your vision will become clear only when you look into your heart.
Who looks outside, dreams. Who looks inside, awakens.

—C. G. JUNG

Chapter 5

Clearing the Ground: Cleaning Up the Junk

Anyone who chooses to tend the soul's garden may realize that it's time to change and that the big changes begin within. The focus on problems moves from "out there" and a desire to blame others to a deep inquiry about how the landscape of one's own mind, heart, and emotions contributes to creating the outer conditions. In India I heard a saying that the path of material pursuits is sweet in the beginning and bitter in the end, while the spiritual path can be bitter in the beginning and sweet in the end. Cleaning up the inner landscape is hard work! But nothing rivals the harvest of peace and contentment it brings.

Working with dreams speeds up the process of spiritual growth. Dreams act like inner films created by the soul-Self where we can watch ourselves and others from a different perspective and discover our shadow side. Like most people, I resist suggestions about ways to modify my behavior when they come from others. But when the scenes come from that cherished soul-Self, the inner gardener, who is filled with loving and kind intentions, dreams often take on deep meaning. The first in a series of dreams arrived to reveal the process.

A beautiful small tree and some packets of seeds sit by a garden fence ready for planting. But the garden is stacked with junk. The fence around it falls apart. The trash stands high and imposing. A woman begins to clear the area and toss the mess into a bin to take it away and prepare the space for planting. She examines the items and identifies old tin cans, jars, and buried tin boxes. She carefully opens the cans and empties them into a compost pile, then tosses the cans into a bin to cart away. Instead of food, the cans contain anger, grudges, greed, and much more. When it looks like a large part of the stuff is gone, more junk surfaces. It seems the work will never end. The space appears dark and in need of sunlight and much attention. The small tree and new seeds desperately need a clear, clean space to grow or they will not take root.

I woke up troubled. I'd spent the day before repotting laurel roses and camellias for the terrace. I loved planting and getting my hands in the earth, so the inner gardener, my soul-Self, chose the symbolic language of gardens to speak to me. Up to me to figure out the meaning. Poor woman! I thought as I reflected on the dream. How could she have so much junk? I'm glad that's not me, I thought. And then I realized that *is* me. The scene represented an image of my inner life crammed with junk! I felt miserable and wanted to cry. I don't have so much trash to clean up, I protested. It can't be true. But without the demands of corporate travel and minute-by-minute reports, I couldn't deny it.

Sitting alone in the quiet I admitted that *maybe* my inner garden required some tidying up before seeds of intuition and a tree of life might take root and grow well. Some junk, like co-dependency, neediness, and whining, had been useful as a child or a young adult. Those behaviors might have helped me to get through tough times and evoke a little pity from family and friends, but now they only sapped energy and kept new, healthy seeds from growing. As an executive, I'd spent so much time working on business objectives and making money that I'd totally ignored the existence of my inner life. The dream added another dimension to the deepening dialogue with my soul-Self, my inner gardener.

I really wanted to ignore the junk and leave the cans closed, but I also wanted to plant good seeds for a better life. The dream intended to help. As I sat on the terrace overlooking the port of Antibes and sipped coffee, I pondered its meaning while the gulls flapped and squawked overhead. I don't like this dream, I thought. But it revealed what needs to be cleared out so that new things can grow. The decaying stuff left behind could serve as compost to nurture the secret garden. I decided to do the work, look at the waste, and embrace my dream life. Then the dreams came fast and furious, revealing every last piece of junk I needed to get rid of. It resulted in so much work to do that I had a hard time keeping up. Maybe my dreams can really help, I thought. I committed to working with them and paid full attention.

The work of clearing arrived in dream assignments, and my sleep time turned into night school. A pen and notebook waited beside the bed, and the dreams woke me three or four times a night. I'd wake up, write them down, and go back to sleep. Each morning I reviewed the images, pondered what they meant, and worked to apply anything I understood. This became exciting, exhilarating, and meaningful work as the subtle contact with my Self, my wise inner gardener, blossomed into a real relationship of teacher-student.

Fear or Flower?

The junk dreams revealed the work to do—forgive people I held grudges against; face fears; stop whining and playing the victim; let go of anger, co-dependency, and addiction to work and coffee. If I cleared away the inner trash from my secret garden during the daytime by being kind, forgiving, and grateful, at night I'd dream of huge trees blossoming with flowers the size of dinner plates. If I fell back into old habits and patterns, I'd find a tree at the heart of my garden withering and in urgent need of care.

Fear appeared like a huge foreboding animal on the loose in the garden. That animal of irrational, uncontrollable dread lurked in corners and under hedges in my deepest psyche, and pursued me until I felt overwhelmed with anxiety and worry. That beast represented fear of ridicule, fear of making a mistake, fear of the end of the world, and especially fear of dying. They all filled my secret garden and killed its newly growing sprouts. I didn't know how to face it or combat that dark animal because it appeared so huge and vague. I felt I should be terrified, but of what?

As a child with a deeply spiritual nature, my introduction to spiritual matters came at a wood-paneled country church with a narrow spire. The pastors instilled fear as they described a story in which all people are sinners marred by a fall from grace and expulsion from the garden. Life led to inevitable hell, unless you lived exactly as they prescribed. But stories from other traditions spoke of the beginning of humanity as an act of love and joyful creation where the Divine yearned for companionship and we return to a conscious awareness of this oneness. "I am One and I want to be many," say the Upanishads.

For some of the pastors in the small church, however, interest in spiritual life could only be motivated by inciting fear and anxiety. "Be saved NOW! Because if you die in an auto accident on your way home tonight without having confessed, you will burn in hell forever," one of the preachers threatened. I shivered with terror and bit my nails to the quick until they burned. There's got to be something more, something better, I thought. I knew in my heart the Divine represented love—not hate, vengeance, and fear.

But fear seems to be a natural human condition still related to our animal nature, and sometimes it's useful. It tells us when to fight or flee and pumps that adrenaline into our blood to rush us out of harm's way. I wanted to lose the animal of irrational fear, the one that paralyzed me and kept me hunkering in a corner in pain. It was only on my trip to India when I met a deeply spiritual teacher that I began to understand and truly tame this wild beast of fear. "The antidote to fear is love," he said, and he showed a better way. It took many years of conscious effort and hard work to practice love, open my heart, and lose the fear. One day after months of hard inner work and many, many more garden dreams, this exhilarating dream arrived:

> *I stand at the garden gate. The fence is mended and it's a spectacular, sunny Technicolor day. Light shimmers on the leaves and on the nearby waterfall. The garden grows thick with vegetables and fruits to feed and delight—fig trees, tomatoes, veggies, and roses of all colors and varieties grow in lush abundance. A pomegranate tree stands in the center thick with flowers, and if it's well tended it will bear a huge amount of fruit.*

I awoke in a state of joy, feeling the promise of accomplishment. If I kept up the inner work, the dream seemed to say, the harvest would be grand. Renovating the inner secret garden of the soul requires many hours, days, and months of concentrated effort. I knew I was set for a lighter, happier journey, but it required more work. As I ventured into the world with the newly cleared inner space, I found myself with so little junk to hide behind that I felt naked. Awareness of the sense of vulnerability struck hard on a London city street where I'd been many times before. But this time, cowering in a doorway out of the view of the crowd, I knew who I had been, but not who I was now, and I wanted to hide.

Clearing Your Inner Space

The invitation to change and grow means taking time to clear out old behaviors, old frameworks, rigid mental structures, and old ways of working that no longer serve. It may mean changing jobs or careers to find a new company that works more in harmony with your renewed sense of values or creating your own company. Or it may mean simply changing your attitudes about your current job, mate, and home. On a sheet of paper you might want to draw images of the junk in your inner garden. Do you have behaviors and attitudes you want to leave behind? Describe what they feel like. When you're ready, shred the paper with your writing, throw it away, bury it, or find a wood-burning fireplace where it might safely burn to ash. As you tear or burn the paper, imagine the junk and the behaviors associated with it dissolving, too. Truly let go of whatever is blocking your way.

Often when we make a resolution to leave some old junk behind, like a grudge against someone or an addiction to sweets or coffee, a test comes to see if we really mean it. We may bump into the person we want to forgive or find ourselves in a situation that repeatedly challenged us in the past. This time, remember the resolution to let go of this ugly stuff and pass the test by truly changing your feelings and attitudes.

Compost: Finding Riches in the Waste

Instead of carting it off, some of the junk and trash might actually be useful as compost. In physical gardens, compost made up of kitchen waste like vegetable peels and peach skins, weeds and lawn clippings, can go back into a heap to decompose and add valuable nutrients for the soil. In secret gardens many experiences and attitudes like pride, excessive ego, and perfectionism can be put into the symbolic compost heap, where they can transform and bring vital energy to nourish art and life. Perfectionism may change into healthy attention to details, for example. What kinds of experiences might you relegate to your symbolic compost heap that will nurture your secret garden?

*You are the pure spirit which pervades this whole universe
and on which the whole universe rests.*

—ASTAVAKRA

Chapter 6

Exposed Earth:
Exploring Vulnerability
and Preparing for Change

Bare earth without all of the junk piled on it may bring feelings of relief and lightness, but it can also leave you feeling exposed. When you cart away old behaviors and attitudes, and turn some roles into compost, it can result in feeling naked and vulnerable. At home I felt at ease and comfortable with my new, clean inner space. Even though nothing much had grown yet, I liked the pure, fresh feeling. But out on the street, no longer dressed in my business suits and stripped bare of old habits and attitudes, I felt like a knight losing every last piece of protective armor. The feelings manifested in a dream:

I'm standing in the middle of the city naked. Everyone else walks around in business suits, uniforms, and jeans. They all look like they're going to work—into offices, trucks, and taxis. But my work is taking me in another direction. When I look at my body, I'm not wearing a stitch of clothing to cover my skin. How embarrassing. How could I let myself be caught out like this? I want to hide.

I awoke in a panic and pulled the sheets tight around my body. After all of the changes, I wondered and worried, "Who am I?" I was once an international business executive who'd spent a lot of time in London, New York, Montreal. But the slick executive persona along with her values died in the Nile. I once fulfilled the role of a wife, but divorce changed that status. I used to identify myself with the things I owned: my watch collection, designer suits, Hermès scarves, and expensive leather handbags. But I'd lost, terminated, or given away many of the things and roles that I'd identified as "me." Now I could wear what I wanted, set my own schedule, and dance to the tune of an inner drummer that no one else heard. A friend called this peeling away the layers of the onion. But when layer after layer is removed, what remains?

Finally, I took a trip to London to visit a friend. I'd traveled there many times on business, but this time as I stood at Piccadilly Circus beneath the racing neon lights, below the double-decker buses, and beside the blaring London cabs, I wanted to hide. All the familiar sights bustled around, but without the armor of my business suit and briefcase, I felt totally naked. I lost the courage to cross the street and venture out into the world as myself. I didn't know who *I* was—and I didn't want anyone to see me without the masks

I'd worn. An urge to hide overcame me, and I sheltered in a doorway while waiting for the panic to pass. Did anyone notice my vulnerability?

The dream of nudity represented a new sense of vulnerability and a deep change in identity and self-understanding. It required digging deeper. If I am not my job, then who am I? If all of these things that I thought I was change, then who am I? Is some part of me permanent? These questions hit kids who graduate from college as they grope for a new profession. They confront empty-nesters who devote their lives to raising children and then wonder about their purpose once this is fulfilled. These questions plague recently retired people who worked long in rewarding careers and then find themselves with time to reflect but no business identity or social status. They hit those of us who fall ill and wonder about mortality. Who am I? Will some part of me continue? This is a mystical question that requires more excavating in the garden to find the first hints of a response.

I held the question in my heart, and once I garnered enough courage, I rushed out of the Piccadilly Circus doorway back to the little London bed-and-breakfast to my shoebox-sized room. I had no answers for these huge questions, and my heart felt heavy, confused, and anxious. If I'm doing all of this work, then where's it leading me? It seemed to be leading me into uncomfortable, new territory where new roads were under construction. I yearned for direction, but I couldn't see the building plan.

Outdoors, behind the hotel, a walled garden protected from the noise and traffic offered sanctuary. I slipped into the silence and felt suddenly at ease among the rose bushes and potted geraniums. I began to breathe in an even, quiet rhythm, soothed by the twittering birds and a gurgling stone fountain in the center. Something lay there inside me, beneath the chattering worried mind, beyond the physical aches and tiredness of my blistered feet that had walked Piccadilly and Covent Garden. Something waited there beyond the confusion, lifting my soul, and it carried me higher and deeper. At the heart of the garden and at the heart of my Self I sensed something vast, huge, beyond my imagination. But I couldn't perceive it or touch it. What was it?

A beautiful thrush flew swiftly past and I yearned to fly like that, too. If an eagle is raised in a chicken yard, it seems it will think it is a chicken. If a tiger cub is raised with lambs, he will think this is who he is. It is only when a teacher, inner or outer, stands in front of us like a mirror and says, "You are *that*," that we can open our eyes to our true nature and soar higher. My inner gardener coaxed me to fly high and know my Self fully. At the moment I lingered in an in-between stage: between the old and the new, and between the material and the spiritual. I felt the earth quake beneath my feet and no ground felt firm. I'd come this far, carted away much useless junk, but hadn't found the new place of peace and comfort so longed for. It seemed the rewards for the hard work up to this point included discomfort and loss of friends who didn't understand. But adventure on any heroine's journey entails moving out of the comfort zone and into new, unfamiliar frontiers.

I sat back, took a deep breath of the fresh, cool air in the garden, and identified myself as an adventurer—a woman exploring a new world in the final frontier inside her own spirit. By shifting the perspective, the discomfort didn't go away, but as an adventurer my feelings shifted to excitement and anticipation of treasures to come. Slipping deeper inside, I realized, "I am not the body. I am not this mind that brings worries." I didn't know really who or what I was, but knowing that I was not fear, nor discomfort nor a business-woman nor all of the other things I'd imagined I was so far, allowed me to breathe easier and grow more at ease with the nakedness. It seemed that by stripping away the armor and mask, my spirit expanded, the doors of perception opened wider and connected me to the huge, vibrant world. With each breath, the outside came into me and with each exhale, that which was within me went out to the world. The thrush must have sensed my ease now because it landed on the back of the bench where I sat and began to sing. Its enchanting song lilted up and lifted my spirits.

My dreams of nudity eventually changed. Joy surfaced as I walked naked through towns and cities waving and smiling at people, not showing off, nor attracting attention, just feeling comfortable and at ease. People waved and smiled casually. All happened in a natural rhythm and flow. Nakedness became a metaphor for transparency, for living without a façade, and being my Self without embarrassment or apologies. No shame, uncertainty, or fear plagued me. I didn't seek to hide my spiritual Self. My heart opened to the people and events that would come into my life. Everything will be fine, I thought. But I was only partway through the journey of clearing the ground in the secret garden, and going on from here meant digging deeper and shaking up the very foundations of my existence. Much more excavating would be required to clean out this messy inner space and allow the new plantings to grow.

Getting Spiritually Naked

The inner sacred space of the secret garden continually changes and evolves. In my dreams it has been a desert, a schoolroom, a place of temples, and a landscape where oversized flowers grow from vibrant trees. It also revealed shadow areas that desperately needed light. In quiet reflection, at a quiet time, settle into the center of your inner garden as the witness, the observer of your life, your actions and thoughts. Ask yourself, "Who am I?" What do you consider most as your identity? Are these things, relationships, properties, career, or something else?

Make a note of the roles and ways that you identify yourself. In your protected secret garden it's safe to set all of these outer identities aside for a little while and take a break. Move into the core of your soulful Self and capture a sense of who you are beyond the material identity. Feel the vastness and expansion beyond your personality. If you'd like, write about how it feels to be spiritually naked. Describe the sensations and feelings you experience. Move deep within and connect with your soul-Self in the heart of your secret garden. The soul's values may differ from your personality's desires. The soul tends to align with the Divine. What do you feel are your soul qualities? Some soul qualities include patience, a love of peace, desire to live in beauty, compassion, seeking to be of service, and many more.

Sharing with a Partner

The journey seems shorter in the company of a friend. On the spiritual journey into the secret garden, sharing with a supportive buddy can help to bring insights. If you like, take an exercise, such as manifesting the image of your secret garden, letting go of junk, or working with recent dreams, and explore it with a friend. Determine you'll each speak about your experiences, feelings, and reflections while your partner listens without making comments or giving feedback for five to ten minutes. Then trade places. Now it is your turn to listen while your partner shares her or his experiences and writing. Listen carefully and attentively with an open heart and mind. Do not judge your partner. Listen with love and affection. Do not speak or interpret during the designated period. This is a wonderful way to develop a deeper connection with a friend and with yourself—and to practice really listening.

The enlarging of the soul requires not only some remodeling, but some excavating.

—NEAL A. MAXWELL

Chapter 7

Excavating the Garden: Digging Up Gems and Bones

Tending to the surface will remove some of the inner mess, but at some point it's time to dig deep. In Antibes, France, across from my sea-view apartment, cranes went up and big yellow machines dug and pounded on the bedrock at the building site beyond my window until one day they suddenly stopped. I knew something curious was going on. The loud men with cranes and hardhats left, and a new, quiet crew came in wearing gloves and khaki pants. The work transformed from heavy banging and scraping with clawed machines to delicate brushing and digging with small spades, sable brushes, and pails. The workers spoke in whispers. One quiet evening at dusk my curiosity drew me to the site. No one was around and I slipped under the barrier. To my delight I saw the remains of the ancient Greek city, Antipolis, buried several feet below the surface of Antibes. I stared in awe at a stone road and the ancient stone foundations of houses.

Well over two thousand years earlier, the Greeks had sailed across the Mediterranean Sea and settled this seaside port. Later, Romans came. The Celts came. Napoleon came. Each layer of history left sediment that settled and needed to be explored for treasures and clues to the past before the new buildings, replete with a walled-off secret garden, could emerge. From my kitchen window I watched the archaeologists pry and probe delicately into the past where previous generations worked, played, ate, loved, fished, drank wine, and produced olive oil. Crawling on hands and knees, their work progressed day by day at a slow, gentle pace that disrupted the building construction and delayed it for over a year.

Synchronicities can be powerful messages. This one marked the beginning of my own period of inner excavations. The outer world mirrored my inner activities. I mined my inner landscape and began to dig up trash, clear the grounds of old hurts, and prepare the inner foundations for new building and landscaping as well. I feared finding dry bones, skulls, and remnants of painful relics from the past. The fear blocked the thrill of excavating the gems. Just below the surface of the conscious self lie levels and layers of rich earthy experiences, dreams, ideas, and feelings to explore. With the attitude of a mystical archaeologist, this is like entering into a quiet, meditative exploration of the hidden artifacts that make up the basis of the current state of the inner landscape.

The civilized world sits on top of burial mounds, ruins from ancient civilizations, and knowledge that has flourished and shaped our minds and souls for millennia. Each past thought, action, and event has led us forward to where we are right now in time. By examining these, we may have an ah-ha experience and understand that the warriors and satyrs dancing on a Grecian urn are lodged in our psyches and our universal memory. We may glimpse some of the fragments that brought us to where we are now and even know some of our past lives.

Some people know they need to excavate, but hesitate. A friend, fascinated by archeology, desperately wanted to understand what blocked her and where her fears came from. She knew she needed to dig down deep and reconnect with her wise heart to find the answers. But she refused. She wanted to maintain the status quo and not get her hands dirty. In refusing to go deep and dig into her inner layers, she cut off her ability to feel her feelings, receive intuitions, and gain insight. Instead she opted for numbness. She yearned to express, create, and live a vibrant life, but until she dug in deep to unblock the creative well, it could not flow freely. She didn't want to risk shaking up the framework of what she imagined to be her stable, secure life. Inside of her burned a white-hot core, like in the earth. She was full of vibrant energy waiting to be channeled into constructive, creative activity. She longed to let go and play. She longed to know and to pray. To find her way she finally decided to excavate. So she began to write, keep journals, and talk openly with supportive friends about her inner explorations.

I needed to excavate too. An illness arrived that required digging deep to find its roots. I knew that the source could be found in attitudes and old patterns. It offered an opportunity to explore the connection between body, mind, and spirit. When excessive bleeding and a cyst the size of a golf ball appeared, I knew it could be serious. The usually surly French doctor who scanned my ovaries using ultrasound made a tiny gasp of surprise when she saw the spot and suddenly seemed preoccupied with my comfort. A week later I ended up in a specialist's office. After the discovery of the images of the black golf ball, I felt rattled. The specialist prescribed surgery. But I went home and decided to meditate on it. As an adolescent I'd had an ulcer and meditated it away in a short time. Maybe this would work for a cyst too.

Lying prone in bed, I placed my hands over my abdomen and imagined light filling the area. I concentrated and went deep into the past. I realized that I hated my body, especially being a woman. I recalled studying the Greek philosophers, who considered women to be like temples built over a sewer. In business I'd become the honorary man and acted like a man in a skirt to fit in. Feminine virtues and values like sharing, cooperation, and compassion get little play in the greedy, political corporate world. Those anti-feminine attitudes reflected my own and the way I'd cut myself off from my feminine, divine Self. But now I needed to dig them out and start over. "I love my body," I repeated. I focused on relaxing and letting the energy of love flow into my body. "I love my feminine side," I said aloud.

The work of an archaeologist is a tough one. It requires careful digging for long, often boring stretches and sifting through dust and debris for tiny chips of pottery and gems. Each recovered item adds to solving the puzzle of what is going on beneath the surface. Each careful brush stroke to the ground removes more of the earth that buries the heart of a mystery. The hours are long; the labor is painstaking under the hot sun. Bringing bones to light may not be pleasant. But once the earth has given up its secrets, once the mystical archaeologist has uncovered her inner remnants and pieced together the puzzle of why she hurts or what made her ill, she can share her discoveries, write down the reports of what she saw and how she felt, and then her world begins to shift with understanding. Bringing bones and gems to light frees the archaeologist in the garden to move on to other places.

During my archaeological dig into my inner landscape, I remembered the people in my life who gave me the impression that being a woman was a curse; the hateful words and slurs against the beauty, power, and grace of women resurfaced. These attitudes lodged in my being, hurt my body, and scarred my mind in the same ways that we scar and abuse Mother Earth. I imagined embracing my feminine qualities of softness, gentleness, and kindness. I held the womanly side of me in my arms and gave her permission to love, live, and express her creativity again. Tears flowed as the memories of the pain surfaced. A hateful relative who called me a whore; men at work who threw around the nasty energy of the word "bitch." I gave myself permission to be a woman with all of the sweetness as well as the strength, power, charm, and the natural intuitive powers that we embody. The well of tears seemed endless and dark as the excavating continued, but finally the pain subsided and a sensation of lightness arrived. When I went for the tests the following week, the cyst had disappeared. I felt elated.

At the excavation site in Antibes, once the archaeologists felt satisfied that they'd found the most valuable items and discovered what they needed to know, they stopped digging. Their work didn't go on forever. They quit and moved on. I hoped and prayed that the construction site would be transformed into a monument, and a park would grow up around the ancient foundations. But ancient ruins lay beneath most of the cities and dwellings in Europe's Old World. So the construction workers got on with their job of pouring concrete, laying new foundations, and landscaping for the exquisite hidden garden. I felt devastated. As an American, I revered all old stones and wanted to preserve them. They should be public property, I thought. I wanted to protest and write to the mayor, but the work continued.

I had a small urge to get special credit and build monuments to the pieces of the past that I'd excavated internally as well. I viewed my inner work with a certain sense of pride. I wanted to erect a special shrine to mark the places in my past that had marked and injured me. I had dredged up painful memories from childhood, actions that I regretted, and memories of people who had damaged me. I saw faces I needed to forgive and how I needed to accept my role in the events that had occurred. I dug and dug a long time and brought many past hurts and pains to light. Couldn't I build a monument to them as well? But like the secret garden and buildings taking shape beneath my window in Antibes, I needed to get on with my life. I needed to move on to other things and start to plant and build now, not dwell on the past or make memorials.

Like the archaeologists, I'd found enough. I'd found all that I needed and it was time to move into the next phase of planting and growing. In a few months a new building and landscape took shape, including a secret garden replete with a spectacular seven-foot-high wooden fence. In a short time, banana trees flourished and water fountains gurgled. For the passerby on the street, this looked like an oasis by the sea. From my balcony above the street, I peered over the fence into the turquoise pools and watched the fronds of the palm trees wave in the sea breeze. Only a few of us knew of the remains beneath the garden. Only a few of us needed to know. No one made a monument to the past, but on top of it they created a glorious, beautiful dream garden where people from around the world come to relax and take refuge. Soon the feminine aspect of the Divine would enter my life and reveal a deeper way of relating to my feminine nature, but she appears in her own time. For now it was time to begin to plant seeds for a better life.

Mystical Archaeologist's Exercise

Sit quietly for a few minutes. Take up your digging pail and turn to the inner landscape. Dig down below the surface; dig gently. Stop. How does it feel? What does the earth look like? What things do you see taking shape under your archaeologist eye? Is it an image? A sculpture? An old piece of pottery? A jewel or bracelet with initials or a family heirloom? Is it an old bullet or an arrowhead? What did it shoot at? What wound did it cause? In your mind's eye continue to dig and explore until you find something inside that attracts your attention. Pay attention. How do you feel about it? Write this down. Draw the images of your inner excavations—a vase, a doll, an old tin can. If you don't like to draw or can't, then create a collage using old magazines, glue, and colored pens. Give your drawing or collage a title.

If you continue to work with the images excavated from your inner terrain, they can become the source of powerful symbols for your writing, art, and creative expression, and also speak to you in your daily life. Sometimes they may appear in unexpected and synchronistic ways. Don't build monuments to your excavated past. Locate the symbols of pain, understand your role in what took place, forgive yourself and others, then let it go. Compost your writing or art that comes from it; bury it; and see what grows from it or find some other unique way to transform it into something beautiful.

Part Two

Planting and Taking Root

"The whole is in the seed."
—Deng Ming-Dao

Just as you would not neglect the seeds that you planted with the hope they will bear fruits and vegetables, so you must attend to and nourish the garden of your becoming.

—JEAN HOUSTON

Chapter 8

Growing Seeds of Love: Planting Guiding Values

After clearing the soul garden of a lot of junky thoughts, behaviors, attitudes, and materialistic values, it's time to plant. The initial junk came from unconscious seeds of thoughts and actions. This time I aimed to consciously choose the best seeds to cultivate. "Sow a thought and you reap an action; sow an act and you reap a habit; sow a habit and you reap a character; sow a character and you reap a destiny," Ralph Waldo Emerson said. What an exciting opportunity to choose in full awareness and to actively cultivate the seeds that would bring a new life. On the drive to the French Grand Canyon, I reflected on human nature and what to plant.

The Gorges du Verdon, the French equivalent of the Grand Canyon, plunges down to a rocky riverbed leaving a gap in the earth. Bordered with tiny, old villages; winding roads; cherry trees; and herds of sheep, it demands a driver's full attention and good walking shoes once you stop. The village of Moustiers Ste. Marie perches on either side of a steep canyon creek, and its chapel appears suspended on the cliff above. Faience bowls decorated with *grotesques* present otherworldly visions of humans wearing wings and tails that trail off into swirls of gold and blue and sometimes transform into plants or animals. The creatures—part human, part animal, and part divine—swirl and dance across the faces of plates and deep bowls. They evoke our origins and deep connection to nature as well as our innate potential to be divine.

On the edge of the town, looking over the stone bridge, I perched halfway between the canyon below and the mountain above, but didn't know where to go from here. Only two possibilities appeared: ahead and up into the unknown or back down the same path where I'd come from. A gold star hung on a forged iron chain strung across the gorge above the town. Placed there centuries ago by a knight of the crusades who had returned from captivity, it bridged the chasm between the cliffs and gave a mystical air of hope to the town.

The knight had left it as a sign of gratitude and recognition to the benevolent divine force that had brought him safely home. The star reminded me to be grateful too for this day with Provençal skies bluer than lapis lazuli and the crystalline light so loved by Van Gogh and Cézanne. But as I tried to find the path higher up, I lost my way. "Do you know how to get to the path?" I asked an old woman in a flower-print dress. She stood on the worn stoop of her stone house. Her smile revealed the absence of a few teeth and of all worldly cares.

"Keep going." She waved in the direction with her hand pointing toward the elevated church. "There'll be signs. *Tu verras.* You can't miss it."

I set out on foot toward a narrow, dusty road that ran midway up the gorge, and soon a herd of sheep crowded the path like low-lying puffy clouds. Dust covered my tan hiking boots and like the coordinated breathing and movement in Tai Chi, each step carefully accompanied my breath. In. Out. So. Ham. Stick to the path. An inner path of course, but which path? Did I need a religion? I wondered. Baptized at fourteen in a font behind the pulpit of a wooden country church, the preacher announced that only people who attended his church would make it to heaven. It seemed odd to me that God would only accept people from this small place. The garden of paradise would be a pretty empty and boring place from this viewpoint.

And besides, why would Spirit birth us all and then accept only a few elitists as companions? Why would the Divine destroy and seek vengeance on the world? I preferred the idea that all that happens in the world is a divine play in which we're all assigned roles. I learned and yearned to see the Divine in all people and things, and even as a child I decided the Divine was an energy of love. Whatever that meant. At the time I read words of the Buddha, Dr. D. T. Suzuki's *Introduction to Zen Buddhism*, and Gandhi's truth and practices of nonviolence, and my explorations brought condemnation.

"You're going to burn in hell," a parishioner assured me.

"I don't believe in hell," I said calmly. But I wanted desperately to find and believe in something greater than myself.

When I picked up the Bible again at age thirty-three, I read that divorce was a sin and I would perish a sinner. On the other hand, Jesus' sweet face and sacred heart contradicted those harsh words as he greeted me in the sanctuary of nearly every Catholic church across France, Switzerland, and Italy. He revealed a picture of compassion and hope.

On travels to Thailand I loved the Buddhist temples decorated with demons and shrines filled with the serene, compassionate face of the Enlightened One. I felt at home and at peace barefoot and sitting on the stone floors while monks chanted and offered food to the gods. In Egypt the Muslims entering their mosques seemed to experience a deep sense of devotion to God that inspired the same in me. And Pharaoh Akhenaten's sun god spoke to unity rather than separation. Akhenaten encouraged seeing forms as many, but God as one. Could any single religion have all the answers for all people and all time? Didn't they all point to a facet of divine love? And most of all, what about this inner path, the one my inner gardener kept pointing out?

My attention turned back to the trail and to a woman in a straw hat who called to her sheep in the distance. Her two big white Pyrenees dogs and a border collie snapped at fluffy heels to keep the sheep together. I caught up with them. "Excuse me. Do you know the way to the *voie des anges*?" I said. The "Path of Angels," they called it. It led along a high road that offered a broad panoramic vista. The young woman perched casually on a rock now; her dogs and sheep lay quietly in a pasture. She offered her dogs water from a fountain that flowed into a stone basin. I stooped to take a drink. She nodded. "Do you want the easy path? It winds up and can take longer. Or do you prefer the harder path that leads you straight to the source?"

Goal-oriented and driven in hiking and even in spiritual pursuits, I asked for the harder, direct path. "I don't have much time," I said. With her walking stick she pointed the way up a narrow sheep path and warned me about an exposed cliff where part of the trail had washed out. Then she sized me up. "It's steep, but you'll do okay."

"Thanks," I smiled. "You spend all year up here?"

"Somebody's got to take care of them," she said, nodding at her flock. A small lamb looked up at her and bleated. "In summer we move around the mountain pastures. In the winter we're confined to the farm. We battle with some wolves, but for the most part, we're at peace."

I'd contemplated how the excessive concern about things and status had brought me to the brink of despair. "Do you envy all those people in the rich houses down below?" Lots of tourists had bought and rebuilt the *mas*, the old stone farmhouses, and turned them into estates in the region. She smiled broadly. "If someone's not happy with few things, it's foolish to think she'll be happy with more," she said. "If she's happy in here," she said, pointing to her chest, "then she'll be happy anywhere."

I would have loved to hear her wisdom long before chasing the empty dreams of all the material goals in business. "What's important for you?" I said.

"Protection, love, and vigilance." She held up three fingers as she marked them off slowly. "Protection means making sure everyone gets home safely." With her long, tanned finger she drew a circle around the herd. "Vigilance means staying alert to danger and keeping it away, and love ..."

I waited, anxious to know more about the mystery of love. She shrugged her shoulders. "No definition for love," she said. "It just is. You know when it's there. And you know when it's not."

I bit my lip and thought about the last few months. My confusion about love versus desire with Kalin had created a painful nightmare and a broken heart. I had no idea really what love meant or how it manifested. It seemed that one of those creatures painted on the Moustiers plates lived inside of me—part human, part beast, and part divine—and the lower, animal part had been getting the best of me. It was the part that responded to lower desires for possessions and for sensual pleasures. "Are you married?" I said.

"Happily," she said. Then the shepherd stepped onto the trail, signaling the end of our conversation. "Bebe," she called to one of the dogs. It immediately jumped to alert, ears pricked high. "*Viens*. Come along." In an instant the herd scrambled up and the dogs snapped at the sheep's heels again. Time to move on. "Think of love like small seeds to tend," she said before setting off down the dusty path. "You tend them by tending to the details in life. The energy you put into a note. The love you cook into a meal..." Her voice trailed off.

"Thank you," I said and set off on the journey again, yearning for answers about that essential piece of the puzzle the shepherd hadn't defined. She loved her sheep with a capital L. She loved her work. It showed in her face, in the softness of her voice when she spoke to the animals, and in the way she tenderly leaned over to inspect the injured ear of one of her pink-nosed lambs. Planting seeds of desires for more money had guided me to a dead end with my job, spouse, and health.

Time to change and think of what values to plant now for the new life I yearned to grow into.

I mentally replaced the dollar sign on my inner compass with Love and started to walk in that direction filled with many questions. What does it mean to love and be loved? How do you work with love? How can I relate to others through love? What does it mean to love unconditionally and to love one's self? What I knew of love—falling in love, parental love for a child, love of my job or of my apartment and possessions—seemed like a limited portion of something far grander and more expansive. If I could get a handle on this one huge ideal, then I would be set for deeper understanding and growth.

On that sunny morning with the skies glistening over Provence, holding the quest for love and the desire to understand it in my heart, some answers started to appear. I stopped to refill my water bottle. Carved into a tree trunk by a fountain along the path, an answer found me in the wilderness. It nestled below a carving of MD + SB = ♥. It read: "Love is energy." My eyes popped. Yes! As I walked and reflected on love as energy, I recalled all of the times I'd said, "I love my work. I love my writing. I love my mother." I sensed that energy present. Enthusiasm accompanies my love of work; passion fills my love of writing; and affection fills my heart when I think of love for family. But the energy of love remained the same beneath it though the feeling and flow might vary. Love is energy, though it may be directed and manifested in different ways.

Deeper answers unfolded on the path. I recalled *The Prophet*. "Work is love made visible," wrote Kahlil Gibran. And I imagined the unfurling of the energy through my body, mind, and soul as I worked and words appeared mystically on the page. That energy transforms into matter through effort. But how will I know when love is present? Will I feel it or see it? I held this question in my heart and continued to walk the dusty path along the cliff. A small mountain chapel lured me in. Angels danced around the altar and plaster doves descended on the Madonna. Jesus' sacred heart leapt with flames of love.

A newsletter printed on pink paper on a wooden table near the door attracted my eyes. I picked it up and the voice of divine synchronicity spoke through it in answer to my question. "Love is patient, love is kind. It does not envy, it does not boast, it is not proud. It is not rude, it is not self-seeking, it is not easily angered; it keeps no record of wrongs. Love does not delight in evil but rejoices in the truth. It always protects, always trusts, always perseveres. Love never fails." (Holy Bible, 1 Corin. 13:4–8.) Maybe when patience, kindness, perseverance, and the other aspects of this recipe take precedence, then work, relationships, and life all fill with love. When I put the best interest of others first, love moves in to take control. I sat down on the wooden pew for a few minutes and closed my eyes to reflect in silence.

The materialistic values I initially grasped fresh out of college focused on gaining more things and pursuing more pleasure. They had guided me into painful and distressing situations that no longer aligned with my spiritual aims. While my role in business had afforded great experiences across cultures and countries, the focus on consuming encouraged selfish thinking rather than service to others and gratitude for what I owned. In relationships the unhappy story had turned out sour, too. I practiced the self-indulgent message, "Think of me and what I will get out of it!" But the more "me"-centered I became, the more my relationships suffered until they faltered and floundered. Would a focus on others and what I can give rather than what I can get miraculously change me and the relationships in my life? Would it bring self-love?

As I looked inside, into my secret garden, I recalled the seed of self-love planted at Karim's recommendation during the inner visualization of my secret garden while in Egypt. Though the sprout above ground had not grown very tall, its roots expanded into the earth. I walked to the side altar where votive candles waited in red glass. Sliding a euro into the donation box, I lit a white waxy candle from a box of matches. That one small flame in this very dark place glowed throughout the obscure chapel with stained glass and dim corners, filling it with light.

Where shadows and darkness prevailed, now a small but brilliant light burned. "Let this be the lamp of love that it may never be extinguished in my heart," I prayed. I yearned to know unconditional love and to sow it into my work. But love is more than a wish and a prayer. It transcends an intellectual idea and finds its reality in practice. The real tests of love were just beginning.

Cultivating Seeds of Self-Love

The Divine accepts and loves us exactly as we are without conditions. Often the hardest thing to grow and cultivate becomes a deep sense of respect, forgiveness, caring, gentleness, and love for one's self. Through introspection we perceive the junk, past errors, and mistakes. Feelings of shame and guilt, suffering caused to ourselves and others, and self-blame may arise. The inner work you do requires courage to see the things you wish to remove and release. It also requires nurturing self-love and acceptance.

Sit quietly for a moment and enter into your secret garden. As you sit here, surround yourself with love and light. Imagine you see a past version of yourself that felt challenged. Go to that self and embrace, forgive, and hold her. Give her all of the attention and kindness you'd extend to a dear friend. Extend an ear and listen to her words. Allow that love to flow back to you and heal your heart.

Companion Planting for Dreams and Values

Wise gardeners learn there's not much need to use pesticides if we choose to place certain plants in proximity for mutual benefit. Marigolds contain natural insect repellent to keep certain pests at bay and protect other plants. Basil planted with tomatoes makes them tastier, and the borage flower planted with strawberries and many other plants naturally protects them from disease. Wise secret gardeners can use similar techniques of companion planting when sowing seeds for their dreams and desires. By dreams here I don't mean dreams that arise from sleep. These dreams well up from your soul and represent deep desires of things you long to accomplish.

Maybe you've always wanted to paint, write a book, buy a place and create a retreat center, host a radio show, or become a massage therapist. By combining dreams with values, your aspirations can take root and grow. Many of us have deferred our own dreams to care for and support others, but now it's time to explore what you want and need. Take a moment to contemplate the seeds you're ready to sow. Imagine your soul desires first. Soul desires are generally from a deeper place within us. They transcend the material, though they may manifest in some material way. What yearnings from deep within you are ready to be planted? Next find the values you'd like to plant as companions to your aspirations and aims. These values may include patience, determination, curiosity, compassion, openness, and more. Defining your values will help to give you direction and keep away pests like negativity. You may want to imagine the values and dreams as flowers or plants.

Once you choose what to plant, contemplate how you would like to cultivate the seeds of your dreams and values in your daily life. Be prepared to put in the effort to make your values and dreams grow. Without effort the seeds will be consumed by weeds or simply not germinate. You may want to take a moment in the mornings to consider how you will cultivate your values and nurture your soul desires. It might also be helpful to set aside a time at the end of the day to reflect on how you fared.

I love to draw my secret garden at different times to see what state the plantings are in. You may want to try this too. Let your hand draw and play without being preoccupied about the outcome. It's for your eyes only. You may want to keep your drawing or a quote that supports your values and vision in a visible place, such as on the bathroom mirror, on your altar, in your office, or in the car to act as a gentle reminder of what you'd love to see grow.

Checking in with Your Inner Gardener

Now that you've been developing your relationship with your inner gardener, it's an ideal time to explore how you feel about this inner guidance. The inner gardener—that wise, higher part of our self—communicates in subtle ways. It may speak in very soft words, through dreams and in visions, or feelings. As you explore your soul connection, do you check in with that wise, inner soul-Self before making big decisions? Do you take a moment to listen to your emotions and feel what they are trying to tell you? Do you go beyond the physical and material concerns to see if the choices you make satisfy your soul-Self, your inner gardener? You may want to take a moment to write out a dialogue between yourself and your wise, inner gardener or simply journal about how this relationship with your soul is developing.

The meaning of life is to find your gift;
the purpose of life is to give it away.
—PABLO PICASSO

Chapter 9

Cultivating Purpose and Meaning

Seekers on a spiritual path often ask, "What am I here for?" and "How can I make a contribution to the world?" Very often the answers arrive unexpectedly in people and places we encounter along the way. After reaching the high path on my outing in the South of France, I headed back down the path toward Moustiers and my car. As the big questions about purpose and meaning wound through my mind, I caught a glimpse of the sheep dogs again. They had nearly arrived at their destination, a green flower-filled pasture up ahead. The giant cream-colored Pyrenees dogs with thick hair over their eyes scanned the field and kept on the heels of the hopping, bleating lambs to keep them together. A small, black-and-white border collie, with tongue hanging to the ground, lay down for an instant of respite. She looked exhausted.

"Keep going. You're almost there," her master said. The herder spoke in a gentle, encouraging voice. Despite the fatigue, the small dog obediently got to its feet and continued the work of herding without a snarl or grumble. The pack of sheep trailed up the final fifty yards to a grassy knoll, meandering right and left in search of choice patches of grass to nibble. A few minutes later, all of the fluffy sheep grazed in the pasture behind a fence. The dogs lay dotted around the meadow, panting heavily in the shade of ancient oaks. They appeared exhausted but exuded a deep sense of tranquility and satisfaction. Their purpose fulfilled, they could rest for the day. It seemed their faces smiled beneath the long hair, and the tired, black-faced border collie beamed with pride and joy.

I envied their sense of satisfaction and accomplishment. The animals knew their job and purpose and they performed well. Now they enjoyed the pleasures of rest after meaningful work. A sheep dog is born and raised to herd, protect, and ward off threats. For centuries it was bred to this mission and it seems inherently aware of it. With training and guidance, the dogs yearn to fulfill that aim. Inspired by their dedication, I reflected on the mission of a human being.

My mind turned to a friend who had a near-death experience after an accident. He saw the tunnel of light, ascended it, and found himself gathered at a meeting around a camp circle. The group asked him two questions: How much have you loved? And have you been loved in return? He said that he stood in the light pondering the question but seemed to have no answer. Instead he returned to the hospital bed with a sense that his purpose was to love. Now, years later, he continues to live with these two questions to guide his thoughts, words, and actions. He lives a conscious life guided by one principle: love. I recalled the phrase I'd seen earlier on the path: "Love is energy." Perhaps if love is God and God is love, then that pure, delightful energy is the basis of everything. To live in the grace of that light, vibrant essence is what I ached for. I longed for Love with a capital L. Not just the romantic stuff associated with sentiment and attachment, but the kind that endures for all time.

Having started my journey into the secret garden, I suspected that the source of that love lay somewhere deep inside; I longed to experience it and also to live with the sense of meaning and purpose that accompanies it when it's shared. I wanted to complete the hard work of inner tending, see my secret garden thrive, and gather the bountiful harvest of satisfaction that I saw in the dogs' faces. That contentment would come if I continued to consistently cultivate my inner garden and act on the divine whisperings in my heart and manifest it in some material way, such as writing books and stories.

While planting trees, strawberries, beans, or potatoes in our family garden patch as a child, I wanted to see the fruits immediately. But the growing process follows a natural rhythm. Strawberry plants take a year or two before they bear good fruit. Asparagus plants take at least two years. Other seeds grow more quickly. In weeks, a month, or sometimes years, if the gardener continues to tend the ground, remove the weeds, and add mulch or compost, the fruits and vegetables may ripen. But only a portion of this depends on the seed. The rest relies on nature or grace, or that energy of love or whatever you want to call the force that makes our hearts beat and the world turn. A friend who plants many community and educational gardens told me that almost every child she works with says to add "water and love" to the seeds. They know intuitively that plants need that mystical, invisible ingredient of love. In my inner garden I knew the experience would be the same. I could cultivate and tend, but the harvest, the final joy and peace, would arrive only through Divine Energy.

I longed to see the results already and find the bliss in my secret garden. I sensed that cultivating the soul would bring satisfaction far beyond any amount of money or material possessions. The fruits of joy would become a harvest that no one could take away. But I also knew that those fruits would not arrive without effort. There was much to do, many seeds to nurture. And like the sheep dogs, I had to respect my nature too. Hindu teachings say that our true nature as humans is peace, awareness, and bliss. Oh, to live in that constant realization! I was born, bred, and grew up with certain inner tendencies and characteristics. Just as sunflowers tend to turn and grow toward the sun, I aimed to grow toward the light and live fully in bliss. A yearning for unity and connection with all things spiritual replaced the empty desire for material possessions.

In the business world, I had started to wither and die, but in a world of people and friends who valued the spirit, I could thrive. If I worked with this self-knowledge, respecting and using it in a constructive way, then it would take me deeper and higher into my interior landscape until the inner and outer merged into one. If I tried to force myself to go against my nature, to return to the corporate world, then it would be like putting the huge Pyrenees sheep dog in a tiny apartment in Miami. It would suffer, turn aggressive and neurotic, and possibly die that way. I'd be back in a corporation in France feeling like a zombie. I wanted to fully realize my true nature of peace and bliss, find the right place and conditions to nourish me, and blossom.

I made a commitment to aim to realize my inner yearning, grow a magnificent secret garden, and reap a harvest to share with others. In a dream my inner gardener felt my longing and desire to waste no time. She said, "You're going to work harder this year than you've ever worked in your entire life." I awoke feeling frustrated, daunted, intimidated. I'd worked long, hard, stressful hours in international business and tossed and turned through sleepless nights. How could inner work be any harder? It was *only* inner work, only the spiritual and mental realms. Without deadline pressures, board meetings, or annual budgets and reports, it would be a cinch, I said to myself. But in my heart I knew my inner gardener told the truth. This inner work would be the real work of a lifetime and bring a real sense of purpose and accomplishment.

Purposeful Living through Tending Your Secret Garden

Clarifying your purpose and meaning can dissipate clouds of confusion and provide direction. Take a few minutes to reflect and write about your life purpose. One way to explore this is through examining what gives your life meaning. Mothering or fathering, doing one's work well, fostering good and healthy relationships, living in harmony with nature and the environment, and being a healer and a healing force can all be a part of one's purpose. Move deep into attunement with your spirit. What's your heart yearning for and prompting you to create? Can you sense a deeper purpose for your life? Can you name it? How do you feel you are fulfilling your life purpose?

Planting Seeds and Letting Go of Results

As you contemplate your secret garden you may begin to perceive a grand design, an overall plan or scheme that helps you to understand some past experiences and get an inkling of what might come. You can plant seeds and foresee a fruitful harvest. But the best work takes place in tune with nature. You may tend your dreams with love and water them with care; you may bring in good energy by planting with kind thoughts and talking kindly to the seeds. But how things grow is out of your hands. The rest depends on the sun of grace, rain of love, and a host of other conditions.

Wisdom brings us to put in effort and cultivate acceptance. As you tend your inner sacred space and watch your garden begin to take shape, is there anything that you need to accept? Is it time to practice surrender to a higher will? Surrender means acceptance. It's a deep wisdom practice that brings a certain peace of mind. The seeds and ideas we plant may not always bring the results we expect, but a sense of faith that things happen to teach us and reveal a higher order can open up a new perspective. In the Indian text the *Bhagavad Gita*, it's said that the wise individual performs actions, but renounces the fruits or the results of her actions. She does not yearn to be recognized for the work or even need to know how something turns out. This means if you render a service to someone, let it go. Don't seek even a "thank you" or to know the end result. This cultivates freedom from attachment and trust in the Divine. But if you do get glimpses of the results, appreciate them and enjoy the growth taking place.

Tending to Your Nature

The sheep dog's nature brings it to herd and protect. Bred and raised for this, the tendencies lie deep in its nature. Take a moment to consider your nature. Settle in deep and connect with your soul-Self, your inner gardener. From this deep place sense your true nature. When all else is peeled away—all of the likes and dislikes, the junk and personality traits—what do you sense? Hindu philosophy says that our true nature is divine. At our core we are truth, awareness, and bliss. In this connected place of purity, can you perceive your true nature?

Empty your mind, be formless, shapeless—like water...
Now water can flow or it can crash. Be water, my friend.
—BRUCE LEE

Chapter 10

Watering the Garden:
Finding the Source

Few things are more essential to life and growth than water. We use water for purifying, cleaning, and sustaining. Many dreams fill with water to reveal the emotions and the spiritual state of being. In mountain villages like Moustiers, fountains pour crystalline water out of cliffs into worn stone basins for drinking. In Antibes, a perpetual fountain runs in a hidden area near the cathedral and the art galleries. It pours into the *lavoir*, a series of stone basins where women once washed their clothes by hand long before machines did the work.

Water holds a deeply spiritual meaning. Posing on the edge of the stone behind the wall that separated this spot from the sea, I thought back to water in Indiana, where I grew up. It lay in still ponds and stood in rain barrels collected by my grandmother in the country. But it rarely ran clear and free like this. Before waterlines brought the source to our door, finding a well required locating someone who had the gift of dowsing or "well-witching." My grandpa, a dark-haired, dark-skinned, exotic-looking man with bifocals, possessed it. He'd acquired a reputation, a high hit rate, and never accepted anything more than simple thanks in return.

"When can you come and find water for me?" A farmer building a new house in Indiana had just jumped out of his pickup truck to the chorus of Mickey, the barking black dog; a beagle; and Grandma's curious goose, Gabby, who waddled around honking. Grandpa shook the man's hand and invited him for a smoke. He loved his old pipe. Just like his father, Grandpa knew how to take a tree limb and divine where the source lay underground. For new homebuilders his gift filled a crucial need. Grandpa hooked a thumb in his suspenders. His dark eyes twinkled behind black-rimmed glasses.

"I'll come on Saturday," he said.

On Saturday we walked into the woods under the young dogwood trees not yet in bloom, and Grandpa found a forked branch on a tree and turned it into a "divining rod." The farmer wanted to build his house where no one believed he'd find water. "We'll see," Grandpa said. He took out his rod, held one end of the forked branch in each hand, and walked around the property. After about twenty minutes he honed in on a spot and walked out and back tracing a grid over it. Each time he arrived at a certain spot, the rod visibly bent to the ground in the direction of the source.

"Wow," I said in my ten-year-old voice. Something mystical happened right before my eyes. It didn't involve machines, scientific instruments, or calculations, but relied entirely on intuition.

"Try it," he said.

I held the forked stick and started a few yards away. When I walked close to the spot, I felt the tug toward the source too, as if it wanted to be discovered. When the farmer dug down about twenty feet, a gush of water poured out. Once they set the well, the water rose with such intense pressure the first days that the farmer couldn't close the faucets in his new house. He let it flow like the mountain fountains in France and Switzerland.

Diviners often say that "anyone can do it." But others say it's a gift. Maybe we all have the ability to be diviners of spiritual waters when we search deep enough. It's like the universe senses our seeking, and mystical avenues and synchronicities open up to respond. We meet a teacher; something resonates with a chord of inner truth; an understanding arises, and we strike deep into the source.

A few years after the well-witching with Grandpa, when I turned fifteen, I doubled over writhing in pain on the ground. My stomach felt like claws ripped at the lining. Waiting tables at a local restaurant combined with the stresses of dating and a tense family environment brought the acid in my stomach to eat at my insides. The resulting pain left me shocked into the precocious realities of life as a teen. X-rays confirmed it. I had an ulcer. The doctor sent me home with a bottle of Maalox antacid, a list of bland foods to eat and others to avoid, and a bottle of tranquilizers (no Zantac yet). After a few days of taking sedatives and floating a foot above the ground, I threw them away and decided to heal myself.

I knew from somewhere deep inside that my mind had caused the problem and I had the power to heal it. Every day for half an hour I sat down, closed my eyes, and meditated. No one in my family meditated. No one had inclinations to Eastern religions. But I knew to sit quietly, close my eyes, and still my mind. Within a month, the gnawing pain stopped. Meditation opened up an inner fountain that cooled the mind and put out the stressful fires. Tapping into the inner well of spiritual energy is not unlike dowsing for water. Water, that fluid, spiritual element, flows up and gives life to everything. But in order to let it flow and remove the block and negativity that caused pain and illness, the mind needed to be trained. The next x-ray proved it; the ulcer had healed. An inner source of calm and wisdom rescued me.

I'm not quite sure how I knew meditation would work. An inner voice said, "Sit down and meditate." I obeyed. This experience convinced me that much of the time we know what ails us and how to heal it. The answers to our physical, psychological, emotional, and spiritual problems often arise from within. If we take the time to listen, pay attention, and act on what our better Self tells us, and take responsibility, we'll have a much happier, more meaningful, and well-balanced life.

The experience revealed the power of meditation, but when my life improved I forgot it again. When the crises hit later and I made the leap of faith out of corporate life, I returned to meditation as a way to bring spiritual waters back into my secret garden and keep it vibrant and alive. Without meditation and the spiritual energy it raised, I couldn't grow.

I needed the inner spiritual waters that arose in meditation to allow the seeds of love, peace, and compassion to take root. This signaled a return to the intuitive wisdom I'd had as a teenager.

When the student is ready, the teacher appears, and that's when I met the Tibetan Buddhist meditation teacher who led me deeper. "Keep your back straight like a stack of gold coins piled one on top of the other," she said. We shivered in coats in a spacious tent at an auspicious site in the hills behind Montpellier. The Mistral wind blew rain through open cracks. The teacher liked to keep the fresh air circulating and didn't seem to mind the chill. I suppose compared to Tibet, where she grew up, this retreat in the mountains in the South of France must have seemed balmy. We chanted Om and sat in silence, ruffled only by the sound of the howling wind. I hovered as close to the electric radiators as I could get without getting burned. Hundreds of us sat silently to experience what the teacher termed the "nature of mind." She struck a brass gong and we took a break from the intense concentration to stretch and relax. Meditation can be hard work!

In a study group with others at the three-week retreat, we discussed what it meant to achieve the "nature of mind."

"The more I meditate, the more polluted the inner waters appear," I said. I thought that spiritual practice and meditation would wash it away. I also thought that I'd done quite enough digging up junk and doing inner work, thank you!

"It's got to surface before it can be flushed out," Eileen, the wise group leader, said.

"So what does that mean, the 'nature of mind'?" a man asked.

"It's a state of bliss. Some people say it's like orgasm," Eileen said. "Only more permanent." I snickered and others guffawed. In spiritual retreats you're supposed to be above thinking about mundane things like sex. "Some people know when they have achieved it and some don't," Eileen added. When we asked for clarification later, the teacher said, "And some fake it." That elusive state of mind meant a place of no mind where all shined brilliant and self-luminous, the teacher said. But unless you experience it, it's just a bunch of empty words. I felt far from attaining any kind of illumination. I just wanted my mind to be still and stop chattering long enough to feel at peace.

At the end of that retreat, the group leader asked me to address the teacher in the customary closing ceremony of gratitude. In front of the crowd my knees shook from nerves and the cold mountain air. The rains ceased and the sun's warmth penetrated the big white tent. It finally started to warm up and feel like June. Someone handed me the microphone as I stood at the teacher's feet. "I came here expecting to clean out a small pool of pollution, but I discovered I need a spiritual equivalent of a waste treatment plant for the toxic waste I've found. Thank you," I said and hesitated. "I think." The crowd laughed. They found it funny, but I knew much, much more work awaited. Inviting in the energy that arrives through meditation brings waves of change not unlike the way a flood reshapes the banks of a river.

As I became more familiar and comfortable with this spiritual energy, I found myself getting very comfortable with this spiritual element—not only diving, but also being able to walk, speak, and even work underwater in dreams. At first the waters appeared polluted, then as I cleaned up my thoughts and aligned my actions with elevated values, they became less murky, until finally the dreams revealed pristine seawaters where I snorkeled and could see colorful, tropical fish for long distances. All of the dream symbols of water spoke to the growing spiritual energy as it rose in meditation. And of course I lived by the sea, a most powerful spiritual symbol of merging with the Divine. But it takes time to learn to navigate in this new element or else you drown. At this stage of practice, when the first joys of meditation and the peace begin to make themselves apparent, one can be easily consumed with wanting to go there and stay for many, many hours at a time. Keeping a balance felt essential.

At the same time, I'd appreciated the Buddhist teachings but wanted more, something that would take me deeper and touch my heart, something that included love. Love didn't come up in these teachings; only a form of it, compassion, surfaced. The Buddhist teachings appealed to my intellect, but I yearned for something that would touch my heart and break open the thick armor I felt there. While the teacher's help deepened my meditation practice, I wanted to go deeper, higher, further, and find that gusher well of spiritual energy, to divine it, and let it flow like the faucets in the farmer's house where Grandpa dowsed for water.

I continued to meditate at the same place and same time every day, and sometimes two or three times a day. Meditation acted to prime the pump and start the water flowing. It seemed I'd found the tip of a well, a small source, and it started to flow. With a taste of the peace it could bring, I hungered for more. The lessons from the Buddhist teacher opened my heart and mind to wisdom and experience from different sources. But I kept my soul's divining rod out, searching and waiting for it to tug and spin me in the right direction to a bigger source, one that would flow ceaselessly. Most of the time my mind raged like a fire in a drought-stricken forest and left me no peace. I needed a rush of cooling inner waters brought by meditation to soothe it and put the fire out.

I also returned to my Christian upbringing and sought more understanding there. Jesus' acts of compassion, love, and nonviolence in a world where he was misunderstood and surrounded by hatred touched me deeply. In meditation while contemplating him, I smelled the scent of lilies and felt his divine presence. But later when seeking answers in the Bible on how to live, I sensed confusion, contradiction, and a language of men seeking power and control. Christian theology provided no gentle place for a woman. It blames us for the fall of man and associates our bodies with sin.

My heart couldn't come to grips with Jesus' compassion juxtaposed with the low place of the feminine in religious teachings. I sought other places, read a lot, and needed more. The meditations continued, but I felt spiritually thirsty for deeper wisdom and understanding. When it seemed hopeless and like the water flow to my secret garden had slowed to less than a trickle, I dipped into desperation. The plants in my inner garden suffered; the inner trees wilted. That's when the divine teacher felt my yearning and called me to visit his Abode of Infinite Peace halfway around the world.

Tapping into Your Spiritual Source

Meditation acts like cool water to cool the fire of mental agitation. While sitting in the tent with the Buddhist teacher, she reminded me to let the thoughts flow past like a leaf down a river. "Stand on the riverbank and become the observer," she said. Thoughts are like leaves or logs that flow past. Don't follow them. Instead, stay put on the riverbank and let them go. This is a practice of non-attachment to the thoughts. Don't become fascinated or frightened by the thoughts. Let them move. Don't block them, stop them, or try to grab onto them. Instead, watch for the space between the thoughts. Focus on that space and expand it.

Observation and expansion are two elements of meditation. While a teacher may guide you to have the right posture and give instructions on following the breath, no one can teach you about the experience. It comes through practice and patience. Only then can you realize the sense of peace and contentment that accompanies the quiet mind. Some people begin a meditation practice by watching the breath or they focus on a candle flame, a sacred image, or a white wall. Some friends find that walking labyrinths or simply walking and focusing on the breath allows them more inner quiet than sitting. Another friend hikes up to a mountain lake and spends hours dangling his fishing line in a mirrored lake and enters into meditation there. Another finds meditation in surfing.

Explore your practice and find what works for you. If you have a sitting meditation, remember to keep your back straight, surround yourself with a protective prayer or light, and stick to a regular schedule. Meditating at the same time and in the same place every day will begin to make it natural and easier. It is like committing to an athletic training. It literally trains the mind to focus. When you get into a regular rhythm, your soul knows that you'll be there listening at that moment. This creates a space and time that aligns you with your spirit.

Finding the Source within your secret garden and connecting with it opens up an incredible, creative flow of energy. Meditation becomes a way to access this, but some people find other ways through art, sports, or service to others, for example. Take a moment to reflect on a time when you have felt "in the flow" and in harmony with your environment and the work or actions you're doing. Can you describe the feeling? What were the conditions when this happened?

When the energy moves freely through you, it brings a feeling of natural joy and contentment. How can you cultivate this experience more often in your life? To connect more with this energy you may wish to write about how you perceive the element of water and how it relates to your secret garden. Making images of it in some way will help you to connect with your psyche and add this symbol as a part of your language. It may then appear more readily in dreams and in symbolic ways in your life.

Don't be ashamed to weep; 'tis right to grieve.
Tears are only water, and flowers, trees,
and fruit cannot grow without water.
—BRIAN JACQUES

Chapter 11

Planting with Color:
Allowing Emotions to Blossom

Working through spiritual transformation stirs up many emotions. In many spiritual traditions, emotions receive little attention. But they can be great inroads to Self-understanding. Getting in touch with them is like planting a very colorful garden that blossoms with many shades and hues in all seasons. So, along with dreams, the meditation practice helped me to train the mind, but it also opened up the raw emotional spaces that surfaced from underground. Spiritual growth can be hard work. Some mornings the dreams brought beautiful gifts and I felt exhilarated. At other times I felt very much alone since few other friends set out on the path with me.

After the Buddhist retreats the teacher's words echoed through me again and again: *Be in the eternal now. Be in the moment.* Like a good student, I contemplated them over lunch with a bowl of creamy tomato basil soup, brie, and French olive bread. I worked to be mindful of each bite. *Be in the present. It's a gift.* But my mind leapt forward into the future and worried about money. What would happen next in my book? When would I meet a good man? "Bring the mind home," I heard the teacher's gentle voice say. "Remain mindful."

"Okay, I will. I will," I said. This should be easy, I thought. I can do this. Just focus on my spoon, the black olives, and the sweet taste of tomatoes. I forced and forced and forced until there was a huge furrow between my brows. The more I forced, the more my mind ran rampant. I exhaled in frustration and took a sip of wine. At that instant a seagull flew past the window screeching, and I was fully present. The bird's screech cut through the mental chatter and opened a space. It sounded like that gull was laughing at my struggle. "Gawk, gawk, gawk," the gull laughed. Instead of enjoying that moment of presence, tears welled up and dripped into my tomato soup. Like it needed more salt! This inner work, planting and cultivating my inner garden, needed to be done in solitude and it felt like hard work. Tired and weary from digging up the trash and bones and letting go of all the old behaviors, I wanted a vacation and to go back to that more exciting life before I'd begun the spiritual journey.

Changing mental habits and elevating emotions seemed tough. It required constant vigilance and effort. I once loved big sensations, strong emotions, drama, and wild swings from despair to happiness. The lower mind thrives on intense emotions, but training it away from the urge for extreme emotional experiences felt tough. It loves the coarse, exciting, painful, eventful ups and downs of life. It loves passionate love affairs and intense relationships that engage strong emotions and bring about attachments. It loves living in the world of TV with bright lights, loud sounds, and strong visual experiences. It thrives on physical thrills, and if it's allowed to rule it doesn't make space for peace. In fact, it finds peace and exploring secret gardens to be rather boring. It cannot appreciate or understand and grasp the subtle, quiet, still inner world of the spirit.

The work to tame the mind and let go of lower desires felt daunting. Would it never end? The tears turned into a river now and left a transparent puddle in the creamy red soup. But I heard the Buddhist teacher laugh. She laughed at herself, at dying her hair to cover the gray because her mother told her to; she laughed at her tendency to grow rounder with age. She laughed at the nature of mind and the materialism in the world. We can work on serious things without taking it all too seriously, she seemed to say.

In my anxiety and pain I recalled the face of a visiting Buddhist monk who had recently arrived from Tibet to the retreat. While the teacher danced and wiggled with her students to the tune of "Twist and Shout" at the closing celebration, the monk sat in his traditional robe on a step above it all, watching with glee. His face beamed with joy. In fact, each time I saw him during the retreat his joy radiated out like the golden rays from Renaissance icons. Though he could hardly speak a word of French or English, all seemed constantly well with him. He radiated joy. I apparently had everything necessary for joy, but still hadn't found it in my garden. Sigh. What was wrong with me?!

In agitation, I opened a book of daily reflections that lay on the kitchen counter. It said that when one begins a meditation practice, she often feels that her thoughts run riot and become wilder than before. But instead of the thoughts and feelings becoming wilder, you become quieter and can see just how noisy your thoughts have always been. Don't give up, it encouraged. Just be present. I felt temporarily heartened and worked harder to focus on the now. But the more I forced my mind, the more it ran away.

"That sounds nice. Right here. I'm right here. One bite. Chew. Chew. Good. It tastes ... I wish I had lobster. I used to get good ones in Montreal. Who wants to be vegetarian anyway?! I can't believe the vendor at the fruit market cheated me out of a couple of euros this morning. I'm a regular. Not a tourist. Tonight I hope Julie arrives on time. She's always half an hour late. Would I be happier if I lived in New York? What about Los Angeles or maybe Beijing? I'd like to see the Great Wall of China sometime." My mind flatly refused to stay right here with me, right now eating one spoonful of tomato soup at a time. This constant chatter wasted so much energy!

Entering into the secret garden to find peace and joy sometimes requires hard work. My mind acted like a little child and constantly demanded that its needs be met, that I pay attention to it RIGHT NOW! I drew it back to the spoonful of soup, where it finally settled a split second. Resting in the quiet just a moment, just long enough for a tiny pause, a tiny space to open up between its ceaseless chatter of words, I breathed a sigh of relief and expected a feeling of peace and serenity. But pain gushed through the space to surface again.

Tears flooded down my cheeks like a spring creek after the snowmelt. Despite the sparkling sea, the brilliant noon sun, the white gulls dancing over the port, and the tourists carrying inflated whales and bright orange and blue parasols to the beach on the sidewalk below, I could not stop the tears. Pain flooded into the present, spilled out into my conscious wakefulness, and cut through hunger, desire, joy. Had it sat there beneath the surface all those years, buried like an old landmine? More pain not related to anything in particular welled up from deep underground passages; tears gushed down my cheeks and spilled into the soup.

"Live in the present," I heard again, followed by more chatter. The sobs ceased. I dried my cheeks, sat down again, and heard the chatter once more. "Nice orange whales. Why can't we go to the beach like they do? The sea breeze feels nice. This soup's not bad, but we've had better. Better than Campbell's at least. You should have made grilled cheese with it like Mom cooked. Remember Mom's? You should call Mom. It's been a while. Collages and magazines for the workshop. Bring the glue. Don't forget it … Live in the present. I want a vacation from my mind!"

I tried to force the internal self-talk to halt, tried to enjoy one spoonful of soup in its full glory, let all my taste buds experience directly and come alive. I'd thought I would enjoy solitude, that I could excel at spiritual practice just as I excelled in studies and business. But controlling the mind and holding back the emotions seemed impossible. When I stopped and looked, great sadness from a broken marriage seeped in along with feelings of abandonment, rejection, stress, and fear brought on by the tremendous changes taking place at light speed.

"What's so great about being in the eternal now?" I said aloud. Tears rolled down my nose and fell into my soup until the transparent pool in the creamy liquid started to look like a small lake. "Okay, now I'm present. It hurts. I feel like crap. What's so great about being here now?"

The witness stepped in. As a writer, there's an awareness of being part of an experience and also being the unaffected witness who watches events happen. I'm convinced we all have that witness in us who remains unaffected by pain, happiness, and changes. It is the eternal, unchanging, and immortal spark of the Divine. Hindus call this *atman*. I also know it as the wise gardener or higher Self. From the deeper place, from the quiet, curious perspective of the witness, calmness arrived. "Everything is perfect. Just look around," the witness whispered, and I felt her peace. "You're hilarious," she said.

I looked up in shock. "How dare you make fun of me." ("Me" being my mind and ego, of course.) "I need sympathy right now," I said. She looked down at me and smiled. Her brightness lit a flame within my heart. Out the window the Mediterranean glowed and shimmered under brilliant sun. Seagulls chuckled and boat motors hummed. Sailboats bobbed past with white, blue, and green sails. Joy decorated my horizon. I sat at a beautiful teak table, eating from antique porcelain and drinking water from crystal glasses. My body had returned to good health. I had no financial worries. I had plenty to be grateful for, so I smiled, stared into my soup that had seemed so dreary a minute before, and then I started to laugh. I am so lucky, I thought. Stop moaning.

The laugh turned into a belly laugh at the ridiculousness of the situation. In the silence of the present moment, a shift occurred. The pain rose up followed by feelings of gratitude for being alive. The suffering had to surface for the gift of joy beneath it to be revealed. Yes, there is a lot of hard work to do, I thought. Yes, it will challenge me to the core and I may not always feel happy, but it's okay to cry. I decided to be content and grateful for the time to do the work and embrace both the pain and the joy that arrived in those moments of awareness between the thoughts. I learned to gratefully accept and welcome them both equally without judging either as good or bad. They both mean that I am awake and alive.

"Wit" makes up the root of the word *witness*. Humor, laughing, keeping a detached perspective helped me to smile even when I felt submerged by the weight of the world and the inner gardening work. Retreats became places to commiserate with others seeking to tame their minds, too. Lots of teachers share stories, and someone told this one:

Two Tibetan monks walk along on their return to the monastery. As they reach a river and prepare to cross, a beautiful young woman arrives. "I can't cross this alone," she says. "I don't know how to swim. Would you be so kind as to carry me across?" The young monk crosses his arms over his chest and shakes his head no with a disdainful look on his face. "I have taken a vow," he says.

"I will help you," the old monk says.

He picks her up in his arms, carries her across the river, and sets her down on the other side. The two monks continue on their journey alone. The younger one broods and

fumes each step of the way. After a few hours the old monk
turns and says, "You seem unhappy. What's wrong, my
friend?" The young monk huffs. "I can't believe you picked
up that beautiful woman and carried her."

"Are you still thinking about that?" the old monk laughs.
"I put her down hours ago. But you're still carrying her
around!"

The story's message of detachment remained a gentle
reminder to put down preoccupations about money, work,
relationships, and even meditation, and leave them behind. An
open perspective invites the universe to play. The whole world
seemed preoccupied with money, me included. One lunch-
time, as I worried about making money in my new career as
a writer, the phone rang. A friend called to announce her next
workshop on abundance. If you think of abundance and focus
on how the world gives so much and always what we need,
then you will be abundant, she said. (And I wondered how she
had heard my thoughts from twenty miles away!) I shrugged,
not really believing it, and went to make lunch.

You've got to work hard and force your way in this world,
my mind reasoned. It's the only way to get ahead and survive. Right? But my wise inner gardener chuckled. I've got a
new way, she whispered. No need to force. Instead, learn to
listen and to put in the effort when needed. Still concerned
about how to marry the spiritual and material, I cracked
open an egg for an omelet and, instead of one yolk, two
appeared. My surprised, delighted laughter erupted out the
open window. I ended up with two eggs for the price of one,
and the universe seemed to be saying, "Relax. All's fine!"

As if this weren't enough of a divine joke, the next day when I went to make a quiche, another egg ended up having two yolks in one shell again! Now, what are the odds of that? With an open mind and heart and a sense of spontaneity, I danced with the cosmos and it danced with me; we moved like two partners in perfect sync. When I listened carefully and followed the rhythm, I could keep pace and stay in the flow. The pain, suffering, and negative emotions fell away and became fertilizer and compost for the rainbow of flowers that began to blossom in the heart of my secret garden.

Creating Your Bed of Roses

While spiritual practice and cultivating a secret garden may not always be a bed of roses, it's still fun to imagine one that you can return to when life seems dreary and difficult. We often refer to a bed of roses as a metaphor for a place of comfort, peace, and love. Using your imagination, what does your bed of roses look like? Is it a flower bed or a literal bed spread with rose petals? Is it a place? Does it allow space for visitors? What kind of emotions do you feel here? Are there thorns to pluck out so you can enjoy it fully? Spend a few minutes writing about your bed of roses. This is also a good time to reflect on your emotional life. Are you connected with your emotions? Do you find healthy ways to express them or do you tend to repress? For many years I have struggled with allowing myself to feel and express emotions and yet not allow them to dominate me. Some people find themselves too caught up in their emotional world and allow themselves to be pulled out of a healthy balance. Which side do you tend to? How can you create a healthy emotional balance?

Choose Joy through Dance

Dancing is a wonderful way to promote and encourage the flow of joy through you. It's a glorious way to connect with feelings, appreciate your body, have fun in community, and get great exercise. My Nia dance teacher reminds me to choose the sensation of joy through movement. Whatever dance style you choose, from belly dancing to tango, Nia, or freestyle, just move whatever wants to move. Invite a form of the Divine that you love into your sacred inner garden to dance with you. Notice the emotions and sensations that arise. Relax and enjoy!

Mentors represent the Self, the god within us,
the aspect of personality that is connected with all things.
This higher Self is the wiser, nobler, more godlike part of us.
—CHRISTOPHER VOGLER

Chapter 12

Inviting the Divine Teacher into the Garden

A good and wise teacher can help make spiritual leaps into higher places. I'd never considered looking for spiritual teachers, but they appeared naturally anyway. My ideal teachers have been like trees—expansive, thriving, and sharing love with all. They arrived often when I reached low points and dead ends. In a dream, the tree of life growing in my secret garden appeared to wither. Trees have long been associated with spiritual life. In animist cultures like Bali, where all things, especially in nature, are imbued with spirit life, trees hold a special place and become objects of worship. In the South of France I'd heard of the healing oak grove hidden on a mountainside in the backcountry and set out to find it for inspiration. Trees can be some of the best teachers. They show how to weather all kinds of conditions, including big storms; they give shelter and fruits without any expectation of return; they take root and constantly change and grow until they become such a peaceful, powerful, undemanding presence that we have to stand back and admire them with awe.

The trees above Les Courmettes, a retreat center and nature preserve in the South of France, required some work to find. The path wound up and around the mountain, then disappeared into a bed of rocks, leaving me to sense the way forward. Sometimes when we trust the intuitive radar, if our soul yearning is aligned with our thoughts and action, it leads us straight to what we need. Off in the distance toward the sea, a storm rolled in from the coast and the fast-approaching clouds required a decision to turn back or continue without certainty that I'd find the oaks. I felt they had to be nearby, so I walked on through briars and over boulders; then with a crack of thunder and a downpour, I stepped magically into the grove of ancient trees. It might have taken four or five people hand-to-hand to hug the largest one. They're an ancient presence that some say is five hundred years old or more, and I thought of how they had witnessed the Dark Ages and the birth of the first secret gardens as they sprang up to offer sheltering walls for delicate and beautiful flowers.

The trees grew miraculously on a hillside, and despite the steep cliff, they remained anchored and strong enough to grow into powerful beings. The peace and serenity in this ancient place signaled its sacredness. The trees gave oxygen like the Divine gives love—without demands or conditions or expectation of a return. I yearned to meet good teachers, ones who embodied these same principles in action, but they seemed hard to find. Teachers who performed miracles existed in other times and places, as when Jesus raised Lazarus, or when the monkey god Hanuman helped Rama build the bridge to Lanka to defeat Ravana. But where do those teachers who perform miracles live today, when only reason seems to abound? Immaculate conception, rebirth, spontaneous healings from dreadful diseases—none of these stands up under the rigid mind of scientific scrutiny, and our world works hard to deny they can exist. But when we allow it, the subtle and great essence of life expands the boundaries of the physical world and miracles become possible.

While on a trip to a spiritual center in Virginia Beach, I carried a list of people who gave "life readings." Some of these psychics could see into past, present, and future, and help to understand why some things happened as they did. Their main mission, I believe, is to connect us with our own spirits and bring healing. Since the insights of Karim, the Egyptian perfumer, had helped so much, I had been intrigued by this ability of some people to "see" and interpret the subtle information that we carry around us, and yet I also felt suspicious. Anyone might make up things that could guide in the wrong direction, I thought. An immoral person might even abuse their powers over another. Some healthy skepticism and choosing carefully felt important.

Sometime earlier I'd dreamed that I had eyes in my hands. I began to pay attention to the ways things felt when I held my hands over them without touching. Scanning like this became a tool to help me feel what foods worked best for my body, what herbal remedies felt right, and what beauty products to use or toss out. I scanned the list of readers with my left hand and found one where the energy felt smooth, even, and peaceful. My flight out would leave soon, but as I stared out the window at the dolphins frolicking and diving in the Virginia Beach surf, my heart cried out, "Call her!" In an act of desperation I phoned Barbara, the woman I'd circled on my list.

"When are you leaving?" she asked.

"In about four hours."

"I'll be right over."

That marked the first miracle. She arrived in about twenty minutes, and we sat in my hotel room while dolphins swam offshore. Barbara's eyes literally glowed as if she stood on a wall peering over the other side into a brilliant white light. "I got here as fast as I could," she said. Given her speed, I wondered if she'd sensed my desperation. We settled in and she turned on her tape recorder so I could keep the session to listen to later. "Do you have something of yours I could hold?" she asked. Some people read palms; she picked up your story through touching an object like a watch, a pen, or something you treasure. I later learned that this is called psychometry. I handed over my amethyst ring.

"So where were you born?"

"Indiana," I said.

"And where are you living now?"

"Antibes, France."

She seemed to look inward and began to speak in detailed pictures as if she saw every important event in clear detail through a camera lens. At first she went way back, even into previous lives. "I can see you in Egypt," she said matter-of-factly. "You were a man putting up symbols on the walls. I don't know if they were tombs or temples, but I see you working with the symbols."

"I've always been attracted to Egypt and went there recently," I said, stunned. Yes, that felt right. Even in junior high history class, I had loved the Egyptians. I thought everyone did. Now she was revealing that maybe there was a deeper reason. Maybe I had once lived there and had good learning experiences in that place. "Symbols are important to you," she said.

"Yes!" I said. "I love symbols."

"You lived in Egypt at the time of the Pharaoh Akhenaten. He introduced you to the idea of the one God," she said.

I sat back in a daze. I'd brought two postcards back from Egypt: one was of Akhenaten, the pharaoh with an oddly shaped body and head whose hands saluted the sun. He encouraged the Egyptians to see the one God behind their pantheon of deities. As she spoke, her words hit chords of truth and simply felt right. They explained my interests in Cairo and the profound emotions of familiarity linked to being there. She spoke too of my family and how they had been people around me in a past life as well. Some of the people I'd met and had the most challenges with involved past-life relationships that sought resolution this time around.

Then she said, "I see your spiritual needs haven't been met." Tears trickled down my cheek as overwhelming feelings of hopelessness accompanied a yearning for that experience of unconditional love. "Have you heard of -----?" She gave me a name that sounded strange and unfamiliar, like cyber-something.

I managed a garbled "No."

"It looks like you're going to explore his teachings, because I see a trip to India for you."

"Alone?" I asked, dreading the thought of so many miles to a strange place without a companion.

"I can't tell. But I think you'll find something there. We'll see."

A spark of hope ignited as she spoke of how the teacher refused money, did not create a new religion, and asked people to serve others, not him. She named celebrities, politicians, and royalty who had visited him, and she described his water projects, educational institutions, and hospitals that function cost-free for those who use them—and patients didn't need to be his devotees to benefit. "For me, he's the best thing that's happened in the last two thousand years," she said. "But I'm not preaching. I don't get anything out of it. You have to see for yourself."

Three months later I arrived to the long lines at Mumbai Airport on my way to his ashram in India. In Western life, we don't make much room for spiritual living. We give space to hard work; it's part of the Puritan ethic that drives many of us to achieve. We permit entertainment in the form of shopping, movies, video games, hard partying, and gourmet eating. We give ritualized moments to a religious service, usually on Sunday mornings. Some people will do volunteer work or participate in charities. Then we feel we've done our duty and get on with producing and consuming again.

In India, the country has a deep tradition and role for spiritual seekers. They're not considered wackos or nutty. Some retreat to ashrams and revere family gurus. Once duties are fulfilled as parents, some even leave family and work life alto-gether to become ascetics who beg for food and wear the tra-ditional orange dress of the *sadhu*, the spiritual seeker. The aim is to reduce worldly desires and attachments and approach closer to the Divine as the body ages. It's considered a way to prepare for death and merge with God. Giving food to sustain spiritual seekers who renounce the world to become sadhus is considered a blessing that brings good karma to the giver. Sadhus may go from village to village and ask for food to keep them alive during their search for God. Though India is adopt-ing more Western ideals, the spiritual seeker is still respected and accepted.

On the bus to the ashram, I met a woman, Suni, who would introduce me to my future home. Suni and I shared a room with two narrow beds and a bathroom. She placed her photos of the guru on the table that separated our beds and bowed in front of it before racing out to the *darshan*. Darshan is the act of seeing the teacher walk among the crowds. It relates to perceiv-ing divine Truth. I turned away embarrassed as she kneeled in front of his picture.

The notion of a spiritual teacher or guru is foreign to most Westerners, as it was to me. We revere self-sufficiency and self-reliance and seem convinced that we can figure things out in a perfectly rational, logical way using the Internet, books, and other research. But reason and logic couldn't provide the experience of unconditional love I yearned for. When I sat on the floor of the temple and watched the teacher walk by, the meaning of love permeated my body, mind, and spirit as an experience. It transcended reason. The presence and energy echoed the feelings of sacredness found in the sacred oak grove multiplied here by a million times.

In the ashram silence, a powerful wave of energy swept through and washed my heart of impurities and pain. Part of the numbness to life had come through carrying a thick armor around my heart, but in an instant it fell away. That powerful energy moved others, too. Tears streamed from the eyes of women and men around me; some smiled and others stared in awe. It was not magic, hypnotism, delusion, or illusion. The presence and energy touched me to the core. It affirmed life, built it up, and made it stronger. I recognized that overwhelming energy as unconditional love and it was not just outside, but also within me. I wept and could not understand how the teacher could give it so freely. I didn't deserve it and had done nothing for him except take up space in the temple and yearn for this experience. This moment brought the withering inner garden into full bloom. That kind of love felt like a warm, gentle sunshine after a very long, hard winter. My inner tree of life revived.

On the temple floor, I sat in the presence of an elevated soul, someone who knew his divine nature. I melted at his feet and wanted nothing more than to be like him, to love and adore him. Feelings like this were foreign to me. Adoration? Devotion? I had felt an inkling of this for Jesus, but not for the religion with all the confusing contradictions that accompanied it. Here I fell to my knees and bowed my head to a reflection of who I am. As I heard many times in India, *Tat tvam asi*—I am That. It's a Sanskrit phrase from one of the ancient Indian texts, the Chandogya Upanishad, that recognizes one's true nature beyond roles and body awareness. The Bible says something similar: "I am that I am."

In a discourse to the crowds, the teacher said, "I am divine." A statement like this would have shocked me, except that the words were soft, sweet, and lacking pride or arrogance. "And you are divine too," he added. Me, divine? Part animal, part human, and mostly divine, he said, and I imagined the creatures on the bowls in Moustiers. Not me, that's impossible, I thought. God is separate. God is out there, distant, something I point to up in the sky. An image on the ceiling of the Sistine Chapel. But the teacher took the finger that pointed out there and up there and curled it around to point it directly at my own heart.

In a dream not long before this trip, I sat on a dusty garden path waiting for a guru to walk past so I could be in his presence. I held my hands together at my heart, feeling deep devotion. The holy man looked thin and wore a dhoti like Gandhi. In the dream he walked slowly toward me. I prepared to prostrate at his feet, but instead, he stopped and bowed to me. I believe he was my inner gardener in another form teaching me this truth: "I am God." The guru mirrors my true nature of bliss and peace. All I have to do is have faith and work to peel away the shell of ego and attitudes that separate me from this wisdom.

The Indian teacher gliding along the path like an elegant angel stole my heart. That thumping, trustworthy organ and the psyche attached to it no longer belonged to me to give to a man or my job, or any earthly thing. It belonged to God— not God that resides in a single physical form, but the divine essence that permeates all of creation. All is one, the teacher said. That's easy to say, but difficult to believe and achieve in understanding. Who wants to be one with the serial killer, or a brutal dictator, or our flawed selves? And yet, the guru said that God is in all and we must seek to see that essence in all.

The sacred and profane are one and the same in the eye of the realized seeker.

I love the Hindu descriptions of how one may believe in and experience God. One can worship the Divine as separate and "out there." Then one begins to feel an intimate connection to the Divine, as if God is a very close relative or friend. *Advaita*, the ultimate stage, promotes non-dualism. The seeker no longer identifies solely with the body, but understands her divine essence and transcends the finite form and name to realize unity with all beings and all of life. This is the ultimate—seeing God in all, experiencing God as the essence that animates every earthly thing from a stone to a toad to a human being. Love opens the gateway to that experience.

Just going out into nature can be a doorway to it too, and invite a deep communion with Mother Nature. But of course all of this discussion means nothing unless it's experienced directly. My ideas formed with more clarity. Love became something practically palpable, as if I could touch it and realize fully when it was present. But my heart was just starting to tentatively open, reach out, and test the terrain. Love, unconditional love of self and others, is hard work. It takes effort and patience. Like trees, it grows slowly with time until it becomes strong and solidly anchored.

As I sat on a cushion on the temple floor, a harmonium filled the thick, warm air and moaned "OM." A *tabla* kept rhythm, and a reed flute pierced the air with a sound of absolute joy. I loved the notes, and by closing my eyes and focusing on them, effortlessly I felt lifted up like a butterfly, elevated higher and wider until my heart expanded. The music grew to crescendo; the reed flute heightened its delight and I swooned like one of Krishna's *gopikas* (cowherd girls), in love with God, in love with everyone sitting around me, in love with the entire world.

This moment marked an extreme shift. From birth, I'd always felt isolated and alone. I never felt I belonged anywhere, and I didn't trust people. I felt like a pilgrim traveling through life, and the only times I really felt connected came in nature. My mantra became "I walk alone." I felt a need to be self-sufficient because I could only count on and have faith in myself. The dreadful, horrible state of humanity condemned us to always be separate and divided. We could never understand or feel the pains in another's heart, nor could anyone truly understand ours.

My photography reflected this. Even while traveling to the most tourist-packed destinations like Las Vegas or Key West, I'd return home with photos of monuments, houses, places, streets, but the photos rarely included people. For me, people meant pain, bad news, complication, and despair. Now, the teacher said that I needed to see God in *all* of these people. And worse (or was it for the better?), my heart was expanding right here to include them in a mind-shattering, earthshaking inner experience where the walls of ego fell away. Oh my God! It encompassed the Indians, Americans, Russians, Indonesians, Muslims, Catholics, Buddhists, Sikhs, Christians, Jews, and all of the other people in the temple and beyond.

To anyone who doesn't have the direct experience, this may sound foreign. Spiritual experiences are very personal and easily snubbed, over-analyzed, criticized, and derided by others. This is why it's usually best to keep them to oneself. Even a few months before, the business-suited, glasses-wearing executive who I was would have looked at me today over those glasses and said, "Uh-huh." Sizing me up as flaky, she would have gone on writing out her business reports and making arrangements for the next board meeting and then made fun of me when she talked to her friends later. "You know, I met this woman today who told me about visiting an ashram and feeling communion with the whole universe. She was really out there." And then she'd laugh and go back to drinking a chilled glass of wine and forget about it. But I sat in a state of ecstasy with my heart bursting with love for the world, sure that love and God exist, and they're one and the same. This marked a huge miracle. I felt alive, awake, and resurrected from the dead. The ashram temple became a physical representation of the core of my secret garden—a place of bliss, joy, infinite peace, and love.

But in a few days I would leave. How do you integrate the experience of universal love into daily life? How do you make it a regular reality? I didn't know and I didn't think it would be easy, but it would lead me a step closer to Home, to paradise in the heart of my secret garden, where I wouldn't have to run to India or any other place to find peace. All I'd have to do was turn inside and *voilà*, I would embody peace and bliss. On the way to the airport, the rickshaw taxi swerved down dusty roads and stopped by the wish-fulfilling tree. Local legend says that the teacher sat under the tree in the early days (before hundreds of thousands of people from all nationalities and religions thronged the place) and asked devotees what fruits they wished for.

The tree bore all the fruits they craved: mango, apple, pear, banana, cherries. We stopped and I walked to the base of it. The tree acted like a metaphor for human desires and our relation to the Divine. We yearn for something and through the seeds of thoughts, energy, behaviors, and actions, those desires become reality. Watch this in action. We plant a tree and then it turns into a giant oak. We plant a thought and it may become a habit; and the habit, if it's constructive and creative, can become what we want. If the habit is writing a thousand words a day, the end result can become a book. If the thought is becoming a chef, then through training, effort, and regular practice we can learn the skills and cook for others. The same applies to spiritual practice. If you want to tend your secret garden and grow your soul, it requires an investment of time, energy, thoughts, and actions. The closer to Divine Energy or love that one is, the more quickly the fruits become manifest in the physical world. But healthy choices about who and what to admit into this sacred space in this critical time of growth will make all the difference in the outcome.

Finding the Temple Inside

The ashram became an outer representation of the inner sacred space. But you don't need to pack up and head off to an ashram or go on a retreat to find the peace and love that appeared there. By going inside, into the depths of your imagination, into the heart of your secret garden, you can find the perfect place for your inner peace to flower and your love to blossom. Find a quiet place, close your eyes, and once again find yourself inside your secret garden. As you walk inside, find the place that to you is the most sacred inner sanctum. It may be a temple, a playground, a place where divine energies flow naturally.

You may find a teacher there in the form of a tree, a person, a divine being, or a presence. Imagine and feel the pure, unconditional love that flows from this place. It fills you entirely to overflowing. Allow your heart to open to receive it. If you feel unworthy or undeserving, acknowledge this and go deeper, to the part of you that welcomes this powerful energy. When you feel filled, come back and concretize the experience in some way using writing, drawing, collage, or some other way to capture the experience.

Bhakti—Choosing the Path of Devotion

In India, holy men and women, saints, and gurus leave worldly pursuits to devote their lives to the Divine. *Bhakti*, or devotion, becomes the sole focus of their lives. Their god or goddess might be Shiva, Vishnu, Lakshmi, Ganesha, Kali, or a host of others. In rural India it's not unusual to see people worshiping cows and trees as well. Their worship is not of the outward form, but of the divine essence the thing embodies, which relates to seeing the divine essence in all and not as a separate entity "up there." Indian women make beautiful, heartfelt displays of devotion, offering up garlands of jasmine and golden flowers to deities. They wait patiently in long lines, often with babies in their arms, to enter into the temple.

Two women displayed deep devotion. With thin bones and graying hair, they sat in front in the innermost temple at the ashram at the crack of dawn. While one played the harmonium, together they sang ancient Vedic praises to God. The hymn called on God to awaken, for if He-She should not, the whole world would disappear. Their song awakened feelings of devotion in me. Devotion combines a complex array of sentiments: love, compassion, gratitude, awe, and joy, to name a few. In the West, we see devotion in mothers, fathers, friends, mates, and lovers. All of these contain elements of the sweetness found in this elevated emotion. Have you ever experienced a sense of devotion? It may be in the way you commit time and energy to a child, to your art, to a mate, or to a spiritual teacher. How might you deepen and cultivate this emotion to expand your heart?

Welcoming Your Teachers

All along life's journey, many teachers arrive. Each imparts an experience or teachings that we can use to grow and expand. The teacher may come in surprising forms—your daughter or son, a partner, a colleague, a stranger on the street—all of them may offer up some insight that will help you to grow. If you choose a spiritual teacher, the best ones will encourage you to see yourself as divine and trust in your inner wisdom and conscience above all. Can you recognize the most recent teachers in your life?

Keep your eyes on the stars, and your feet on the ground.
—THEODORE ROOSEVELT

Chapter 13

Taking Root for Growth:
Staying Grounded on the Journey

In ancient times, yogis and yoginis (spiritual seekers) retreated from the world to live alone with their spiritual practices. The Indian ashram offered an easy place to be at peace with few cares, and I so wanted to follow their example and stay there for a long time. But modern yoginis don't have that luxury. We're called to be in the world, remain centered, and stay grounded. But after India's deep spirituality, the return to the French Riviera provided an amplified jolt.

No two worlds contrast more than India and France. In India, women cover themselves with yards of elegant silk fabric that make up their saris, while up and down the coast from Nice to St. Tropez, bare-breasted women sunbathed on beaches and expensive, white ship decks. The sun beat down by day and techno music beat out from the port bars and clubs by night. After long Indian days of silence, I wanted to hide in the cool, sheltered space of my French Riviera apartment. From where I stood with the eyes of India, Antibes' streets looked filthy from lack of rain, too much greed, and excessive desires for material things. Of course, little had changed here; the transformation instead took place in me.

When I dared to venture outdoors on the port one late afternoon for a walk in that less-peopled interlude between the afternoon's packed beaches and the sortie of night creatures, I ran into trouble. I'd felt fragile, broken open, and raw since the return, and I avoided seeing friends. I slipped outdoors during the quiet times when I'd be least likely to encounter anyone. With the scent of Indian jasmine still filling my nostrils and visions of India's giant butterflies still in my sights, I walked past the expensive yachts in a daze. The journey had taken me further and further inward, away from all that had seemed so real and important before, into a realm where the inner world started to seem more real and alive than the outer one. I floated above the earth and didn't really want to come fully back into my body.

But to anyone looking from the outside in, I appeared the same. I'd not spoken much of the trip to friends. When Adrian, a hot-headed American, drove up beside me in a brand-new convertible Mercedes sports car, unaware of my recent travels and transformation, I knew it signaled trouble. He appeared so proud of his new acquisition, and I felt happy for him. "Hello," I said and smiled. Still dazed and dizzy from the return to high-speed civilization, I walked on. Adrian drove beside me at a slow pace. "Hey, how's it goin'?" he said. "Good," I said but felt transparent, fragile, and as though I was floating a foot above the ground. After the Indian experiences I felt as if the shell around my heart had broken open even wider than at Piccadilly Circus. With so many barriers stripped away, I wanted to stay up in the clouds and not deal with the everyday stuff. "All's fine," I said. I continued to walk in my ashram daze.

In the ashram, the day before I left, a strange, inexplicable event occurred. As I sat on the temple floor in Bangalore, the holy man walked among us. The open-air temple held a small crowd, and an enormous statue of a blue-skinned Krishna perched at the back. I held my hands at my heart and savored the last moments in this blissful territory and dreaded the return home. How would I ever reconnect with this peace and bliss back at home in my portside apartment? "This is just a taste of peace," the teacher said. "But real peace and bliss are within you. You don't need to come here to find it. Take it with you wherever you go. It is your birthright and your true nature."

His words referred to the sacred space within, to my secret garden. But it seemed impossible to cultivate it so the peace and joy would remain constantly well rooted. In deep concentration I watched the teacher's head as he walked among the crowd. In an instant, a flash of brilliant white light came rushing out and permeated me. I sat stunned on the thin cushion. When he left the temple, the door where he exited flew open as if by magic and he disappeared, but the effects of the ethereal light remained. I sat practically paralyzed on the floor, unaware if anyone else had experienced it.

The temple workers began to sweep away debris and urge stragglers out. I was the last one there and struggled to stand. I wobbled away, still feeling the stunning power of something that I could not and still cannot explain. Was this a flash of grace? I weaved my way across the chaotic, dangerous Bangalore street, between the three-wheeled rickshaw taxis and the more dangerous four-wheeled ones, and sprawled blissfully on the bed at the hotel. I never, ever wanted to leave. I loved India. I loved its spiritual light. I loved my teacher. I loved love.

But life goes on, and I ended up on the port with Adrian beside me expecting a compliment on his new car to bolster his ego or else he might attack. I floated slowly and felt love for him, yet I couldn't come out of the quiet, dazed place and speak. But he insisted. I felt him demand a compliment on his car as he drove along at a walking pace beside me. But his car just didn't seem very important compared to the bliss of being in my secret garden. When I remained in the reverie among the blossoms of my growing inner garden with a peaceful smile, he couldn't take anymore.

"Well f ... you!" he yelled. His tires squealed as he sped away. To my surprise I did not react. The whole business left me totally unaffected. That's when I knew that a profound change had occurred. When other challenges and potentials for conflict arose, the same thing happened. I remained calm, quiet, and unaffected while those around reacted as they wanted. Before India I might have returned the anger and hurtful words. But this time my heart remained still and unruffled.

The spiritual sustenance from India acted like sun falling on seeds ready to take root. It gave a spurt of growth to my inner garden of peace, which now needed some protection. The teacher said that peace and bliss is everywhere, and India gave me a glimpse of this reality. Now it was up to me to cultivate my inner terrain until those seeds matured. During this delicate time it meant putting up temporary walls of protection and allowing only a few like-minded people to share my experiences.

As in any natural garden, the first plantings require special care and attention. Conditions must be right for growth to take place; the garden needs proper rainfall, temperate weather, good soil, and plenty of light. In this garden of the soul I carefully cultivated that deeper connection with my Self. In daily life this translates into finding spiritual-minded company, cultivating deep friendship with oneself, reading sacred texts, and spending time in nature and other sacred places. I no longer chased after money, designer clothes, or luxury restaurants. Instead the inner garden became my priority.

Another dream arrived to mark the shift and draw attention to the company I kept:

I am with two friends in rising waters. We are on what once was expensive Riviera real estate, but it's mostly underwater now. We swim toward a mountain peak to escape from the flood. A woman who feels proud of her big house and beautiful possessions and a man consumed with self-centeredness call out to me. "Save me!" they yell loudly and flounder in the water. I swim ahead, rapidly approaching the mountain, but turn to look back and assess the situation. I realize if I try to save them I will drown, too. I swim on ahead and leave them behind.

Both friends in the dream represented aspects of myself I needed to leave behind; they represented the quest for material things, feelings of disdain for others, and selfish desires. I could not bring these companions along on my journey to oneness and peace because they thrived on separation and selfishness. Even though these friends functioned as symbols, they also embodied those energies. Living consciously, we see the realities and choices that need to be made. I realized they would not and could not understand or support my changes. We could no longer dance together. Time to move on. But I needed good company and the right environment, and the Riviera couldn't provide a good place for spiritual growth.

I also struggled with forms of the Divine. I'd picked up a photo of Jesus in India. In my meditations, he stared back at me with dark, liquid eyes and I felt guilty for adopting other teachers as well. Was it wrong to revere more than one teacher? I wondered. And what about the Buddha whom I loved so in tankas and temples? Should I eliminate the small statue of him that I'd picked up on my travels? As if to answer my despair, a new dream arrived to help me reconcile it. Jesus stood before me, arms open, smiling. The Buddha and the Indian teacher arrived too. Together, surrounded by light, they merged into one divine light without form. When I awoke, I felt blissful, quiet, and certain that religions and forms are many, but God, Divine Energy, Love, Great Spirit, or whatever you choose to call it, is One.

Soul Friends

Good company fed my soul. When I befriended people who also shared a spiritual journey, I felt uplifted and found sustenance. But when I found myself in the presence of people who cared most about money, cars, and things, and valued these over people, I felt drained and emptied. With some people it seemed they literally sucked the life out of me. But in a crowd of creative, spiritual-minded people, I felt mostly energized and supported, not criticized. Who we keep company with will make or break us on the spiritual journey. And in my experience, it's sometimes better to be alone and practice in solitude if you can't find a supportive spiritual group.

Amid these deep changes and transitions on the journey into the secret garden, many friends could not venture very far with me. Those who wanted me to stay the same felt threatened by the changes. But I couldn't stay there just at the entrance to the garden. I needed to continue onward and circle toward the center. A friend who considered entering into her secret garden recently asked me, "Can you hold on to colleagues and friends when you change?"

"Maybe and maybe not," I said. She wanted to head in a new direction, but sensed this meant taking risks. "You or they may make other choices. We don't all grow and blossom at the same time," I added. I thought of friends from Alcoholics Anonymous who struggled with change. When some of them became sober, their partners protested, preferring the weak, addicted, sick person to the one who healed and became strong. The same happens with spiritual growth and healing. Some friends and family will feel safer to see us with our weaknesses and addictions and aim to maintain us in this place rather than support our growth and encourage us to expand and change.

Change threatens many people. Some may leave us as we grow, or we may leave them behind. Cultivating non-attachment helps. Love the moment and the people and things in the moment. Respect and appreciate them. But don't be attached to them. If they go—as all things will eventually—then that is the way of life. The Hindu goddess Kali teaches this. Her name derives from the Sanskrit word *kala*, which means "time." Time will consume all material forms eventually. Enjoy the present and let go of what no longer serves your spirit's life. This is easy to say, but the practice requires deep commitment to your soul-Self.

Staying Grounded

When going through big spiritual changes, it's sometimes easy to move into those elevated and rarefied spheres of the spirit and allow the soul-Self to stay "up there," but it's vital to stay grounded, in the physical body. We can keep our head in the clouds and our hearts connected to the Divine, but the feet need to be firmly planted on the earth. Some ways to keep that connection include walking barefooted on the ground and wearing the color red, a root-chakra color associated with physical vitality. Get your hands in the earth and plant something, weed the lawn or garden if you have one, and walk on grass. For a grounding visualization, imagine your feet rooted into the ground and reaching down into it like a huge tree. Feel the earth's energies move through your body to bring in vitality, nutrients, and energy.

Symbolic Relationships

Life is reflection, reaction, and "resound." The people and events outside of us are often reflections of things taking place within us. They can give clues to understanding our inner workings. I cringed when a pompous friend showed up strutting around in a dream. At first I suspected my mind was playing out nightmares. Then I realized this spiritual truth that life is like a mirror. My friend merely reflected back an image of my own deep insecurity. Once I realized this, I worked on my insecurity and let it go by building spiritual self-confidence. Each time she showed up again in my dreams, I knew I needed to work more to overcome this inner obstacle.

The two friends who drowned in the dream as I swam to the mountain peak also symbolized characteristics that I chose to leave behind. They included the quest for material things, a sense of superiority, and a pursuit of self-serving desires. I perceived that those characteristics drove their actions. Other people who showed up in both my dream and waking life reflected strengths and qualities. For example, the appearance of the U.S. president in my dream life referred to the executive, the part that takes action. Different actors I embrace or "get in bed with" in dreams usually represent a facet of charm, humor, or talent that I seek to acquire.

If you'd like, take a moment to list your friends, enemies, and important people around you. Beside their names write the key qualities and/or weaknesses that they represent for you. Which of these qualities would you choose to develop more? What weaknesses would you like to leave behind? During the next days and weeks, keep these in mind and consciously work to develop the qualities and diminish the weaknesses.

Part Three

Tending the Secret Garden

The true source of all spirituality is within you.
Know how to use the time to grow.
—Deng Ming-Dao

A garden needs constant maintenance, as does our relationship
with whatever god or gods we wish to worship.

—RONI JAY

Chapter 14

The Inner Gardener's Allies and Enemies

Every garden contains pests as well as beneficial creatures. The wise gardener helps to identify them and determine what to do next. The mind often points to other people as the nuisances, but the real enemies in my inner garden slouched in the shadows and lingered under the bushes inside of the secret garden of my soul. Aphids of anger and mites of greed, together with selfish desires, envy, jealousy, and hatred, wreaked havoc. I pointed a finger and said, "They came from out there. We don't have that kind of junky stuff in here."

My pain and suffering are the fault of my ex, those difficult people around me, and my boss, I thought. But when those people weren't around and my secret-garden roses still struggled to survive because of the infestations, I finally admitted that the real problems originated inside the garden of my mind. Time to work with my inner gardener, that higher, wiser part of my Self, and get out the pesticides of love. My inner gardener and I had a little meeting and determined that, though it would be easier to blame others, I needed to take responsibility and control the ugly irritants.

I took the microscope inside to examine them. Off in a corner well hidden beneath the leaves, aphids bore dangerously into the roses. Unstopped, the May rose with its precious scent, the oleanders, lavender, and jasmine would succumb to their destructive powers. Though practically invisible, each aphid reproduces every day, creating millions of pests over the summer, all gnawing at the beautiful flowers until they die. The garden becomes a war zone. Big efforts like vigilance, weeding, pruning, and careful tending are required to protect the delicate plants and allow them to grow. Aphids resemble low-level anger—niggling, tiny, almost imperceptible until they ravage and take over a whole area of leaves and kill off the creative life of the beautiful flowers attempting to blossom.

"I never get angry," I said, in total denial. But the secret gardener urged me to settle in to work. "I'm so fed up with this inner work," I yelled at her.

"But yelling and getting angry at them is not going to serve any purpose," she said. In the face of her inner calm I decided to pull at weeds and inspect the recent damage to the plants while that shadow part of me who wanted to blame others reflected and scratched her head.

"But if I could only think first before speaking and reacting, then I might preserve some relationships," I said.

An anger infestation arrived when a close friend casually invited the man I was dating to her house for dinner and a massage. I demanded to know her intentions. Of course I talked to my date, too. But to preserve our friendship, I asked to speak openly to my friend about the situation and clear the air. She wouldn't answer my phone calls for a week, but finally we scheduled to meet. She showed up late and brought a group of friends along. Her avoidance stirred up more anger until I felt my view of her misplaced intentions around my love life was true. My ire filled the room with sparks and hot explosions of energy as I spoke.

"When you play with people's intimate relationships, you're playing with fire," I said loud and strong. When I finally felt drained, I left trailing a red streak of fire. It felt important to release the anger rather than keep it bottled up inside. But most of us have not been taught healthy ways to do this.

Much later, a teacher taught me to release the anger by allowing it to move up and out of my body. When that energy stays blocked, it brings illness and suffering in its wake, but as it flowed up and out, I felt the surge of power and even some pleasure associated with it. The teacher told me how she had recently gotten angry at someone and when the anger came, she recognized it and said, "Stop! I want to feel the anger." She then allowed it to rise and enjoyed it. Once the moment passed and she cooled down, she addressed the issues with her colleague in a calm, clear-headed way. I love this approach! In it anger is not bad; instead, it brings a message. It's allowed to flow, and then once it passes, the situation can be addressed with serenity.

But back then I felt embarrassment at the way I released it. It erupted unconsciously and out of control. Desire, attachment, jealousy, and frustration lay at the root of it. But it brought with it an opportunity to learn and grow. Later when I spoke with my friend, we apologized to each other. But our friendship suffered permanent damage. Anger can be used constructively to move us out of bad situations and into better ones. But the way the anger is expressed demands awareness, care, and conscious attention.

Anger can turn the inner garden into a war zone, waste time and energy, and destroy all in its wake. Where I allowed anger to take root and thrive, it choked out beautiful new growth, damaged relationships, and brought out harsh words that caused deep wounds. Wounds caused by harsh words of anger may take longer to heal than any physical wounds. Weeding out this pest requires vigorous and determined efforts. I needed to recognize when and how anger crept in and then release it in healthy ways. This time the anger came from irritation, from expecting desires to be met and then finding them frustrated. I watched it creep into others' gardens and destroy them too, but sometimes I found it harder to see it steal silently into my own sacred space.

Other pests hung out and required watchful attention. Envy and jealousy, like slugs, could eat away at the beautiful, peaceful interior. If they found their way in, they'd chomp at any plant that might be nourishing and nip it in the sprouting stages until it withered. Keeping an eye on them required careful reflection and contemplation. They snuck in, often in the form of criticism of others, and corroded the garden's fences. Lust and desire thought only of getting what was good for themselves; and greed built up the ego into an overblown, separate, self-centered cockroach that took the biggest strawberry in the patch for itself.

Identifying the invasion of these pests marks the first step to exterminating them and the damage they're doing in the secret garden. It's practical, get-your-hands-dirty kind of work that most of us want to avoid at all costs. Most of the pests are related to the notions of "me" and "mine." They connect to ego desires and a limited sense of self that identifies "me" only with my body. To destroy them, the pesticide of self-control combined with guiding values and strong doses of love, patience, and persistence help. Keeping the mind elevated and focused on the Divine acts like a ray of sunshine.

Regular gardeners know of the long hours required to treat and prune their roses, weed out the bad plants, and prune fruit trees to ensure a good harvest. The inner garden requires the same attentive care. In deep examination of the inner space, the inner gardener must look at what pests lie in wait, and work with them through vigilance and conscious thought and action. By kicking these obstacles out of the inner garden it will flourish; and when the internal garden blossoms, the external world will also thrive.

Pesticide to Kill Anger Aphids

To cope with the anger aphids in the garden, I learned to practice presence of mind and to step back and look at a situation before reacting. This is sometimes easier to say than to do. It may require walking away from a situation and returning to it later with a calmer mind to address what stirred up the strong emotions. Anger aphids burn like fire; they overrun the garden of peace in an instant if I am not vigilant. If someone raises her voice or provokes, I remember one teacher's words: "Putting out anger with anger is like putting out fire with fire."

By not reacting with a loud voice, harsh words, and door-slamming, the atmosphere remains calmer. When these pests get into my sacred space, putting them out requires great efforts of time, patience, and presence. They overrun the place mercilessly and destroy the plantings that thrive. I cope by moving away from the place where I feel bad, taking a deep breath, and moving inside to the sacred space in the heart of my secret garden. Inside I focus on something soothing: a quiet song, a mantra, a place in nature where I feel blissful. The best way to cope with anger is not to let it enter in the first place, but once it comes in and sets the garden on fire, then it requires immediate attention.

Douse it the same way you'd put out a fire—drink a glass of cold water. Take a deep breath and think carefully before speaking. The choice about how to release anger comes from within and can change through conscious action. With grace, I may be able to take a step back, look at the funny expression that anger creates on my face, and laugh. I combat envy and jealousy through feeling joyful for the success of others. By expanding my heart, their joy becomes my joy. Gratitude becomes a constructive response along with reflection on all of the wonderful things in the world around us.

A challenging moment arrived when a friend announced his engagement. I felt a twinge of envy and wondered why I had not yet had the fortune of meeting the man of my dreams. In my heart the loneliness welled up and brought a tear. My friend's joy glowed through his eyes and he felt happy. I congratulated him and sincerely opened my heart to wish him all the best. Though I yearned to meet the right mate, I learned to appreciate my time alone, cultivate friendships, and surrender to the divine will within—the One who knows best about timing, events, and the right people who bring the right life lessons at the right time. My voice of wisdom, my wise inner gardener, whispered up from the depths of my heart, "Befriend yourself. It will all eventually change. Practice being content with where you are and who you are."

She usually spoke less, but I guess I needed more encouragement and instruction this time. "Peace in your inner garden relies not on obtaining physical things for satisfaction, or on relationships, but on mastering yourself and living by inner guidance," she said. I sighed deeply and dreamed of that time in the future when I would marry, too. I knew it would come. But time in the garden is a strange and immeasurable thing, and I hated waiting. She smiled, soothing my anxiety. "Will it be long?" I said.

She placed a soothing hand on my heart and whispered, "You have more work to do first." I wanted to cry. My heart felt split between yearning for a deeper connection with the Divine and a strong desire for a spiritual partner to share the journey. Couldn't life include both? I asked my inner gardener. Eventually, it seemed, but not for now. This part of the path required doing more work in solitude. "Have patience," she said. "The answers will unfold in time."

Watching for Pests That Kill the Best in Human Nature

The main pests that invade the garden of human nature are greed, anger, hatred, lust, envy, jealousy, and desire. When these deadly insects enter into the heart, they destroy the blossoming and growth of the human spirit. Most of these pests take root in desires for status, material things, a relationship. Take a moment to contemplate. What pests, if any, invade your secret garden? Become conscious of them, but don't focus too much time and attention there. Focus instead on developing the allies like peace, compassion, and kindness that will help combat them. The allies come in the form of your guiding values and love. They act like natural pesticide. What guiding values and attitudes do you need to cultivate to help you combat the enemies in your garden?

Draw or write about which allies you plan to cultivate in your sacred space to maintain equilibrium. If you like, share these with a trustworthy partner. Some of the allies in the garden include love, peace, truth, compassion, doing the right thing, nonviolence, and other soulful qualities. By cultivating these in place of the pests, the secret inner garden can thrive. At the end of each day, take a moment to examine your secret garden and the progress you've made.

*What we experience in dreams ... belongs in the end just as much
to the overall economy of our soul as anything experienced
"actually": we are richer or poorer on account of it.*

—FRIEDRICH NIETZSCHE

Chapter 15

Renovating the House in the Garden

Dreams, more than most any other spiritual practice, serve us to develop the garden of the soul. Through dreams we're given insights into our shadow self—the dark side that haunts, threatens, and inhibits joy and growth. Dreams reveal the side that we often don't want to see or can't face in the light of day. They also introduce us to intuitive powers, give warnings, and provide protection from other negative influences and from ourselves.

Regular periods of meditation help to tear down the barriers between the dream and waking worlds. As dreams flooded in, I dived deeper into dream work. Except for Freudian theories that had boiled dreams and humanness down to a beaker of sexual desire, I knew very little about what went on beneath the surface in sleep. Why do we need to be unconscious for six or eight hours, or about a third of life? What happens then? Not satisfied with textbook explanations and wary of books or people that might tell me to do it their way, I ventured into that final frontier using inner guidance. I have a deep faith that each of us has access to profound inner guidance (that I call the inner gardener here), and this is our best teacher. Dreams offer one way to access it.

At first, becoming aware of that netherworld wasn't unlike diving. When I moved to the Riviera, the thought of swimming in the Mediterranean Sea aroused terror. I imagined demons, monsters, and mysteries beneath the surface. I'd tiptoe into the blue-green waters off of the islands of Lérins, where white jagged stones, sea grass, and sand plunged from ankle-deep to depths of over six thousand feet. I'd flirt around the edges going only as far in as I could see into the transparent waters. But fear kept me from going deep, until one day when I garnered the courage for a "baptism." That's what the French call the first dive.

With a mask, flippers, air tanks, and a belt of lead weights, a guide pulled me sixty feet underwater for my first view of that hidden world. This environment had a life of its own that had remained entirely unknown to me until the dive. Squid communicated with colors; moray eels with rows of jagged teeth and hearty appetites snaked through sunken ships; sharks the size of cars ate plankton; jellyfish, octopi, and fish with razor backs and wings glided into crevasses and underwater grottoes. Conger eels lived in sunken World War II boats and slithered around anchors of ancient Greek ships where amphorae of olive oil and wines once scattered across the sea floor.

A whole new world opened up below the surface. The life there had been going on all along—eating, breathing, reproducing, and recreating—but this was the first time I'd become aware of it. Fascinating, shimmering with decreasing degrees of light, beautiful and scary. I was out of my element. Without special instruments I couldn't see and breathe, but if I had a mask, flippers, and tanks, and paid attention to the rules, followed the decompression steps, and stayed close to my buddy and guide, I remained safe with nothing to fear.

On inner dives into dreams, the same rules applied. Pay attention; stay close to the guide (my inner gardener); set ideals and aims that encourage soul growth; remember my value of love; and remain practical. The first inner dives revealed murky water, lots of pollution, darkness, and waste. It required special efforts for the inner cleanup. The first dreams of trash marked only the beginning; more images and scenes flowed as fast and furiously as rushing water, and the work got tougher. I consciously made the commitment to learn from this inner source and to understand it. My wise gardener obliged and continued to wake me several times a night. After dream cycles I scribbled down the images on a notepad by the bed, then fell asleep for more. The dreams revealed pests in the garden, and my inner house appeared a mess. To guests in my Antibes home, all looked *Elle Decor* perfect. By the sea, full of windows, blue sky, and azure sea views, the white sofas, silk pillows, and carpets married in perfect harmony.

But the house in my inner garden beneath the sea of consciousness revealed another picture. The psyche uses many symbols to communicate, and this time it used the metaphor of a house. The house, for me, represented the residence of my soul. In my first house dream, shutters fell off; weeds grew in the yard; brown patches and dirt appeared where grass should grow. An old swing with peeling paint hung on the porch, and weathered, gray, bare floorboards needed serious renovation. A screen door barely hung on its hinges. Inside it looked worse, with a stained, tattered sofa. Newspapers and old files lay on the floor, and pictures dangled sideways next to yellowed, moth-eaten curtains. A yellow police tape roped off the basement, warning not to enter, and rotten steps on the stairs to the upper floors kept me from ascending.

"Pay attention to your inner renovations. You need to do some serious housekeeping," this dream said. After years of neglect, this house needed desperate attention. But what did that mean for me in waking life? The cleanup started with moments of reflection and self-examination. I seemed like a workman entering the house to check out what parts needed mending. The inner workman demanded a mental clearing out.

Get rid of the demons of depression; stop numbing out; transform attitudes of playing the victim. They all contributed to a rundown inner state. My focus turned definitively from looking at others as the source of miseries to seeking the cause more deeply inside. A 180-degree shift of perspective! Huh, you mean I'm responsible for this place being so rundown? I thought. "Yep," my inner voice answered gently. "Time to get to work."

"Okay, got it," I said. By accepting responsibility and no longer blaming others, I realized I had the ability to change and the power to make my inner world better. A huge discovery! I am responsible for my inner world. I allowed the inner house to decay, but I can build a palace if I'm prepared to do the work. And so the hardest work I've ever done began. I continued to watch my mind chatter on in meditation and let it flow past. I recalled the retreats where I learned to meditate and calm the mind. During a spiritual retreat I watched myself and others and became amazed at how, despite teachings that included compassion and kindness, our egos clashed as we continued to put ourselves first. Waiting in line at the retreat cafeteria seemed to bring out egos at their worst as people jockeyed to move in front of each other and struggle to get in first.

It revealed the difference between intellectual understanding of spiritual principles and dedicated practice. It's easy to listen peacefully to the teacher with his soothing voice and sit quietly in his smiling presence. But turning the teachings into practice posed real challenges. My little self still screamed, "Me first," just like a first-grader. But watching it helped me to say, "No, let others go first."

My family and friends became my teachers too, and almost every situation provided an opportunity to learn and tests to verify that I'd understood. Most of the work came in daily interactions. As I examined some relationships, I found they involved dependency, abuse, and addiction. I tore the police tape from my inner house and went into the basement to reconnect with lost memories that had been the source of these relationship patterns from childhood and beyond. And then I changed.

Some friends preferred the rundown house, the old me. One of my changes required learning to communicate. When something bothered me, I'd keep it tightly locked inside, stacked in my interior closets, and let it seethe until resentments built up. I held on to anger at a good friend who didn't invite me to her party; my ex who had chided me for keeping the house "hotel clean"; my family's reticence to pick up the phone and call me. In my personal life I felt there were two ways to communicate: to be obsequious or to bark out commands. I learned that displeasure, disagreement, and wishes could be spoken of softly, but still be expressed. In some cases they needed to be voiced to avoid the buildup of bad feelings and misunderstandings, and to help others. My usual response of brooding silence brought no solutions.

A new house dream surfaced:

I'm in a basement apartment filled with clutter. Chairs lie on their sides; a table is overturned; papers spread across the floor like a whirlwind just blew through. Little light enters the skylights and windows. But I feel comfortable here. I live here. In the next scene my wise gardener—the higher, wiser part of me—stands beside me at the entrance. She glows, smiles joyfully, and invites me in to see the changes. Someone has painted the walls white, straightened and aligned the chairs as if they await a symphony orchestra, and stacked all the documents neatly. In the center of the room, a huge crystal vase of red roses stands in a ray of light on the table. Sun floods in. Every detail is beautiful. I turn to my guide and say, "I liked it better the other way."

When I awoke, I realized my deep foolishness. I didn't really prefer the mess. I simply felt more comfortable in the mess than in this newly renovated inner space. I laughed at myself and continued to renovate, though sometimes the frustration made me want to cry, too.

Over time my dream house changed. Instead of the dinky rundown house, sometimes I lived in a house with an attic where I walked up the stairs into the light. Sometimes a sparsely decorated white marble dream palace with many rooms awaited me. My house holds many mansions, I thought as I opened door after door to new experiences of expansion. A glass-walled greenhouse filled with lush tropical plants represented a state of transparency where I could see out and others could see in. I had nothing to hide. Sometimes the houses sat on hills or by the sea, and recently I moved into a lighthouse. Inside my secret garden all of these houses belong and reveal stories about my state of being.

This kind of inner work requires effort and courage, but if you choose to do the work, the rewards and the treasures you will bring back include greater peace and contentment, more self-love, and a growing Self-awareness. You may know the expression "As within, so without." This mystical equation reflects spiritual truth. Ultimately, the results of the inner work begin to show up in the world around us. Instead of experiencing relationships with wild ups and downs and mad drama, they become deep, rich, and rewarding. We move into emotional and intimate territory that brings connections which transcend the physical, depend less on appearances, and rely more on the vibrant and stimulating soul-to-soul contact with others. As the inner garden transforms and blossoms, the physical world will begin to reveal new and much more rewarding experiences.

Inner and Outer Housecleaning

In parallel with my inner renovations, I literally renovated and cleaned out my apartment and closets, which had been stacked high with stuff. Towels, unused clothes that I saved for Sundays until they were out of fashion, photos from travels, old administrative documents. I cleared them out, organized them, and gave away what I did not use. The less I possessed, the lighter I felt. The junk piled up in my home weighed me down. But cleaning became a form of meditation.

In India, some gurus teach that cleaning can be used to focus on polishing the mind and clearing out negative thoughts. I'd watched women at an ashram in Andhra Pradesh rise at four a.m., perform prayers, sketch their auspicious chalk drawings at their thresholds, and sweep the ashram clean of twigs, palm leaves, and coconuts that littered the walkways. Sweeping away dust became a metaphor for removing debris from the psyche. In their devoted concentration, the cleaning provided a powerful symbol for correlating the inner and outer experiences of the world as well as a practice for concentration. What kind of inner and outer housecleaning, if any, are you prepared to do?

Your House of Dreams

Carl Jung, the renowned psychotherapist who worked with dreams, literally built his house of dreams. He received a series of house dreams and felt the creative urge to materialize what he saw. The house, built over more than twenty years, sits at Bollingen near Lake Zurich, Switzerland. Its rooms represent aspects of himself. Made of stone, it includes a tower. "From the beginning," he wrote, "I felt the tower to be a place of maturation—a maternal womb—in which I could become what I was, what I am, and will be. It gave me a feeling as if I were being reborn in stone." He referred to it as his symbol of psychic wholeness.

Many people dream of houses and connect with them as symbols. To explore the house as a symbol, begin with where you live now. What does it say about you? Is there an area that you love most? Which area do you avoid? Is there an area that's particularly cluttered? Take a few minutes to reflect on this and perhaps write the thoughts that come to mind. Next allow yourself to slip into that dreamy, creative space where the mind is relaxed and playful, like a child with a calm focus on her favorite toy. Think of what your dream house might look like. What might it reveal about your inner state of being? What kind of inner renovations and house cleaning does it need?

Inside your house of dreams, what does your most sacred space contain? An altar, a place where you can go away from the world to rest and contemplate? What symbol might you find in this space? If you like, create an altar or a sacred space inside your physical home where you can keep this symbol to remind you of your inner work.

Checking in with the Secret Garden

Have you kept a regular schedule to visit your secret garden? You may want to return to your first writing, collage, or drawing of it. Check in and see how it grows now. In a quiet moment of reflection or meditation, enter in and observe how it appears. If you like, make a pre-dream suggestion to dream of your secret garden and see how it grows. Try another collage or write about it. How do you feel about it now? Have your feelings changed? Remember the secret garden can be a wonderful place to renew your spirit. If you don't visit it regularly, what obstacle is keeping you away?

Heroes at this point are like mountaineers who have raised them-
selves to a base camp by the labors of testing, and are about to
make the final assault on the highest peak.
—CHRISTOPHER VOGLER

Chapter 16

Expanding the Garden:
Setting New Boundaries
and Entering New Space

Sometimes the inner gardener will challenge you to grow
beyond your boundaries and move both spiritually and literally into new places. As I sat on my balcony in Antibes watching the sun rise over the port, a watery dream resurfaced that
did just that.

> *I see a map of the coast from above with colorful fish float-*
> *ing on the surface. The fish lay belly up from Monaco to St.*
> *Tropez. Some fish flick their tails in a last effort to push*
> *themselves back down into the water and fight off death.*

A few fish remain alive, but are in danger of catching the disease that killed the others. It seems the waters contain toxins and cannot nourish these rare and beautiful fish.

Learning personal symbols and how to work with them becomes part of the fun of working with this inner world. I felt like a detective trying to uncover the clues and follow the soul guidance. Fish. What did they mean? On dives offshore I recalled how few fish populated the Mediterranean. The Greek fish symbol came to mind and I associated it with spirituality, nourishment, and water. Fish live and breathe in the ocean. They thrive in clean, healthy water. But the fish in this dream lived in polluted water. As I worked to dive inside and find clues about my life, the waters in my dreams changed from murky and polluted to clear and populated with vibrant sea life including fish, dolphins, and squid. Water and particularly the sea came to mean a spiritual element.

From the terrace in Antibes where I watched the sun lift out of the Mediterranean Sea and tint the water pink-gold, the seagulls flapped and screeched their excited approval. But off in the distance toward Nice and the airport, a gray-green smog hung over the towns. In another two hours the roads of the city would be clogged with traffic. The thought made me cringe. I walked around the port, and a few dead fish floated next to plastic Evian bottles and McDonald's bags between the million-dollar yachts. It looked like a mirror of my dream. The Fort Carré, the star-shaped fortress, ruled over the sea and town like an ancient temple. But all around for miles, the land stood barren and dry from drought.

Local flora included parasol pines, a few yuccas, lavender and laurel rose bushes. But more and more concrete walls, streets, houses, and apartments left less and less space for people and nature. The Riviera suffered from a drought not only of rain but also of spiritual energy. Just as the plants suffered from a lack of rain, I suffered from a drought that came from lack of a spiritual community. I thought back to the dream and the map, conscious again of the pollution, and understood the message. Time to move on, it said.

The realization hit home with a shock and resistance. The ego-self prefers habits and comfort of familiarity, but the soul-Self urges us to move into new and better places that will make us grow. But growing isn't always easy. I loved living by the sea. Haven't I made enough sacrifices and changes for now? I thought. Can't we slow down and enjoy this a little? I wanted to protest and bargain with my inner gardener for more time and for a little fun along with the hard work. Let's negotiate a way where I can stay here and not let my growing spiritual life die like the fish in my dream, I said to that still, inner Self. But a knowing rippled through every cell of my body: time to move. But to where? The logical place would be back home to the United States, where I knew the culture, could get back to my native language, and find myself in familiar surroundings. But that didn't feel right, so I continued to weigh the idea and look around.

Holding only a feeling about an impending move, the preparations began. Mental preparations came first. My apartment contained over fifteen years' worth of photos, antiques, and collections of LP records, watches, and more. I weighed what to take and leave behind. I also sought out friends who shared a longing for spiritual growth. One friend found her needs met through tarot cards; another resorted to mediums; and another friend preferred Alcoholics Anonymous. But none of these provided the kind of regular support and encouragement that I needed in this delicate period of growth. The Riviera appealed to a certain type of individual—one more like the person who I had been, someone who was attracted to wealth, gourmet restaurants, sunbathing, the sea. The coast once set the scene like the backdrop in a play for my more materialistic life, but the next phase required a new setting.

While in India, I dreamed of moving, but thought of it as a spiritual move, an inner move.

I am with my mother (not my birth mother, but a maternal form of my inner gardener), a white-haired, older woman, who accompanies me. We walk together through the streets and she points out to me a white cross sewn onto a red fabric. "It will be beneficial for you to go there," she says. I feel happy as we drive now through the streets toward this new place where the land is green. I think maybe I will meet my future mate at this new place. A thrill of excitement and anticipation rushes through my body. The new place has palm trees too.

What could that white cross mean? While contemplating it on a walk, I saw the white cross on a red fabric exactly as I'd seen in the dream. It was a Swiss flag hanging in front of a bicycle shop. Would I move to Switzerland? I knew almost no one there, except for Suni, a woman I met in India. She lived in an obscure part of the country near Italy where they spoke Italian. When I called she suggested a stay at a lodge in a remote valley for a few weeks to try it out. She lived a short drive away.

On the trip from Antibes, past the Italian Riviera, past the smokestacks and the port of Genoa, through the plains planted with rice, over the Po River, and into the outskirts of Milan, excitement of adventure stirred through my bones. Frequent tunnels and demanding, curvy roads on high cliffs marked the beginning of another journey and paralleled my inner travels. At first I entered long periods of underworld darkness punctuated with moments of blinding light. Each instant demanded constant vigilance to remain safe, all while speeding along at eighty-five miles an hour. Not much different from the spiritual life!

When the verdant foothills appeared outside of Como, a few miles from the Swiss border, the trees, grass, leaves, wild thyme, and violets embraced me. The green mountains felt like old friends, and the emerald colors resonated with the hues of my heart. It presented such an extreme contrast to the dry Riviera! On the arid coast, gardens grew only with great amounts of irrigation and careful urging. Here green appeared everywhere. I rolled down the windows to take in the fresh air and feel the coolness caress my face. This place promised paradise.

Trading in my thin silver sandals and other luxuries of the Riviera for hiking boots and a more natural and simple life came easily during the first months. My boots and backpack itched to be called into service. At the end of an Alpine valley I rented a monastic room with wood floors, a single bed, and a bookshelf. The days split between writing and walking, meeting the salamanders, admiring chestnut trees, and learning new languages—one of the Italian-speaking Swiss and the other of the soul. And I immediately started to climb.

Getting to know the mountains requires time. It's a new level of the garden, an ascension to a higher vista. When the ascension begins, the first few feet will find you panting heavily unless you've trained in the mountains. At first only the surrounding houses and cars, and maybe a piece of the parking area or a picnic table, come into view. But climb a few feet higher and the body begins to adapt to the new rhythm. Shapes of the valley start to come into view. Reference points change and the larger patterns of how things fit together down below reveal themselves. The higher the perspective, the greater the overview of the terrain below.

From the refuge on the mountain peak above Bellinzona, clusters of houses and the highway spread out below. The river narrowly kept to tamed banks; the valley tapered at the mouth of the old city where two castles perched. The landscape shaped the places where the inhabitants of Ticino built houses, with more homes on the sunny side and fewer on the damp, darker side of the valley. The deep mountain waters of Lake Maggiore, split by an imaginary line on the map, showed no sign of pledging allegiance to either Switzerland or Italy, but belonged resolutely to both. The tiny islands of Brissago and the larger Italian Borromeo Islands struggled to keep their shoulders above water. From above, all became visible in its beauty and perfection.

On a first hiking trip up Monte Generoso, I trekked alone from the tiny village of Scudellate at the end of the Muggio Valley and found a rarely used path that disappeared between *rusticos*, old stone houses, and animal stalls. A yellow sign indicated two hours to the top. One foot in front of the other, I climbed the near-vertical incline past goats that stood on the path and stared, past the bony-backed Swiss dairy cows. On the Riviera, the sea provided ample opportunities and metaphors for the watery subconscious, but the mountains paralleled new physical, mental, and spiritual territory.

Climbing to higher vistas became symbolic for moving into a higher stage of spiritual awareness. Few people choose these paths. They require stamina, fitness, and determination. About halfway up the mountain, the peak seemed farther out of sight than when I first began. The path snaked back and forth in long curves, and hikers converging from another path strolled leisurely along. I couldn't figure out why they would waste so much time meandering back and forth on switchbacks. I looked up past the cows munching in the pasture and decided to go straight up, over the tall clumps of grass, past an old stone ice house, straight to the top.

Why waste time? Full of energy, I sped up to the peak, where a rainbow ring of light surrounded the brilliant Alpine sun and snowcapped peaks spread out far into the distance. When the sun slipped in the sky, I reluctantly left behind the views of the high peaks, but knew I'd be back for more. Something clicked in the silent nights watching the glimmer of shooting stars trail across the clear skies. At night, a deep peace descended and the air allowed impressions to flow in easily. I longed to make this area my new home at least part of the time.

I decided to return home to Antibes and make preparations to move. An art of working with inner wisdom is learning the importance of timing. My get-it-done business mentality meant that I found a place to rent in Switzerland for the summer and immediately wrote a letter to my French landlord announcing that I would move out of the Riviera apartment for good. I had no plans beyond the end of the summer. I popped the letter in the mailbox, and later that night I dreamed this:

A small, rash boy of about ten years old takes charge and I find myself out in the cold. He's cute, blond, but does not see ahead very far. He acts on impulse and we're both left outside with no place to live.

When I awoke I knew I had made a huge mistake. Though I still planned to travel to Switzerland, I called to cancel the letter (which the owner graciously accepted) and kept the beautiful sea-view apartment. I realized the subtle difference between knowing something must be done and waiting for the right time. Many people might not need a dream to paint a picture of rashness, but I sometimes found it difficult to strike a balance between my head and intuitions. By this point I felt deeply committed to following my inner guide even if understanding all of her subtleties required patience. I sought the right balance between surrendering to the inner life of seeking and practical living in the material world. Striking this balance meant proceeding like a tightrope walker. Acrobats on the high wire walk a straight line and move forward with great concentration. They hold a long balancing pole, making minuscule, barely visible adjustments to maintain equilibrium and stay on the wire. If they lose concentration, stop focusing on the next step, and let their mind wander off to what they'll have for dinner, then chances are they will fall. I worked hard to keep my balance.

In Switzerland, I met spiritual-minded friends, and many of them also hiked. Making the climbs with them, both physically up mountainsides and spiritually into new levels of awareness and integrity, seemed easier. One of them, an experienced mountaineer, trained me to keep a steady, even pace. The switchbacks were there for a purpose, he said; the paths laid by Alpine trekkers decades ago followed the contours of the terrain, avoided dangerous cliffs, and conserved energy. I'd chosen the tough way to the peak the first time, going it alone straight to the peak of Monte Generoso without following the switchbacks; but from then on I followed the wisdom of a steady pace and also applied this practice to my spiritual life.

At these altitudes whole farms moved into elevated summer pastures at four to five thousand feet; rocky paths crisscrossed the peaks, curved into spectacular valleys, and revealed high pristine lakes the color of blue-green emeralds. All of this life of cheese making, herding, and views of an occasional glacier happened far above the world. I loved stretching out in the sun and relaxing into the grass while the bees danced from edelweiss to blue gentians and wild, red azaleas. On my own I would never have gotten so far or discovered some of the most beautiful rivers and waterfalls.

Sometimes on the path, new hikers would race past us in a furious hurry and we'd catch up later to find them collapsed under a chestnut tree already out of steam, while a steady pace carried us to the peak. This can happen with spiritual stamina too. Despite the aches and pains and the difficulty of learning a new sport, patience, perseverance, and a sense of purpose drove me on. The guide sometimes let me keep the pace, but he also watched to make sure I didn't surpass my capacity, climb out on a rock cropping, or step on an icy snow patch that might send me shooting off a cliff. With a steady pace we worked up to a much bigger conquest—Monte Zucchero.

After regular practice, one foot in front of the other during most of the summer, we set out in a small group for the ascent up granite cliffs to the 8,975-foot peak. That altitude might seem small to some, but given the sheer granite cliffs and the steep elevation gain, it required some tenacity and skill. In sacred texts and mythology, gods often appear as rewards for effort in these transcendent heights and transmit messages of wisdom and reassurance. I waited and anticipated that if we made it to the top, they would greet us there too.

In the morning chill, we climbed the sugar-cube-square rocks up to the pass. The divide revealed both sides of the valley spread out below. Only two of us continued up the narrow, rocky, slippery cliff. One woman kept looking down; though she had the ability to climb, fear and vertigo held her back. Others waited at the pass due to aching knees, fatigue, or lack of desire to go on. The steep rocks required careful attention to footing, but in less than an hour we stood on the peak.

At that instant an eagle hovered in the air before our eyes. The mountains and glaciers spread out 360 degrees, and petty cares of the world far below fell away. The eagle turned, circled, and floated up on the air currents. Without batting a wing, it soared higher and higher, into the highest cumulus clouds until it became a dark speck, and finally disappeared into dizzying altitudes. Tears of joy filled my eyes and my body shivered with pleasure. The eagle with its acute vision sees clearly from a high perspective and with barely any effort ascends into the heavens. With a wingspan of five to seven feet, it is associated with freedom and possesses the ability to soar to great heights. Native Americans revere the bird as a sign of the soul that carries prayers and brings strength, courage, wisdom, and illumination of the spirit. It rises far above the material world to perceive the subtle, spiritual elements. It sees the overall pattern, represents power and balance and higher truths. And it urged me to ascend even higher.

Expanding the Boundaries

When you leave behind the need to impress, to consume a lot of things, to create emotional dramas for yourself and others, you're beginning to enter into the higher vistas of your secret garden. The mountain climbing mirrored inner efforts to climb into a new space of creativity and expansion. The air is rarer here. It's a path that few choose to travel and you have to listen closely to your inner guide to find the way, your way. A hawk may screech and signal to watch for the signs. Watch for opportunities to expand, grow, and move to higher views and see the *bella vista*, the beautiful view.

In your meditation, during your quiet time, scale the inner heights. Ascend the peaks of your spirit. Leap off beyond your usual mental confines and let the wings of your soul carry you to a broader vision of life. Breathe in the air here. How do you feel? What judgments and criticisms can you leave behind? What limitations and shackles can you let go of to make your ascent into the higher levels of the soul easier?

I can hear the deep silence any time I remember to listen.
It's right below the noise.

—PENNEY PEIRCE

Chapter 17

Finding Grace in the Garden of the Spirit: Making Friends with Silence

Some parts of life's journey require us to go it alone to inner places where no one else can come. It appears like a withdrawal from the physical world, but paradoxically that move eventually takes you deeper into union with others. To anyone on the outside looking in, it may also appear self-centered, but at its best it's divinely Self-centered. My heart yearned to move into deep communion with the Divine, and I felt that presence most profoundly in the quiet of the mountains.

In a little Swiss mountain village, I spent twenty-one days in silence to listen intently to the inner voice. No conversations, no Internet, no words slipped through my vocal cords. No TV. No music. On business travel as an executive, I turned on the TV immediately when walking into a hotel room. A room filled with noise and moving images chased away feelings of loneliness and kept my mind on the surface. I didn't know how to spend quiet time alone or even want to. At home in Antibes, I reacted the same way. Enter the apartment and grab the TV remote control, turn on music, or pick up the phone to call someone. The silence threatened and aroused a sense of anxiety. But what did I fear? Getting to know myself?

It took time to make friends with silence. At the Buddhist retreat before the Swiss move, I became conscious of my aversion to the quiet and examined it. The teacher requested that mornings be spent in quiet contemplation. She meant no conversation. She banned cell phones, Internet, TVs, and radios from the site. Nestled in the hills of southern France, the mistral wind whipped the prayer flags and howled through the grand tent. Some people could not bear silence and chattered in loud whispers on the paths at the outskirts of the center. Some seemed to feel a fear of annihilation without a constant stream of words exiting their mouths. But in those serene hours of the morning without human voices, the crickets and cicadas hummed, the birds chirped, prayer flags flapped in the wind, and water gurgled over rocks in a narrow creek. The silence fed my soul, though it didn't give me respite from my mental chatter.

While on the Riviera I experimented more with silent practices and sometimes spent whole days without speaking. Sundays naturally found me alone and usually on a hiking trail in the Gorges du Verdon (the French Grand Canyon) or in the high lands of the *arrière-pays* off of the Riviera. On those days, leaving home early, I'd head down the winding roads that led to Moustiers and wound around the edges of the gorge where fluorite-colored waters flowed in the rivers and bikers wearing skinny tights whizzed around the curves. In the silence with only the car's motor whirring, my mind focused on the present, on the crystalline light and the purity of the cloudless skies. Often hiking paths beckoned me through caves and out along the river. The silence enriched the space and made the experience of light, vibrant Provençal colors and gray stone walls a deep pleasure without distractions.

Later, on a hike with friends in the Swiss snow at nearly 5,500 feet, the silence greeted me again. We stopped for a break. A thick layer of fresh white snowflakes in the middle of the Alps blanketed the area in a sound-absorbing quiet. But between the four of us chattering and the crush of our rectangular-shaped snowshoes against ice, we could not hear the silence until the pause. I requested that we stop speaking for an instant. No planes crossed overhead. No cars roared in the distance. Even the cascade held still, frozen in glacial blue shafts. The profound silence enveloped us in the sparkling diamond light of the snow. It permeated me with a joyful wonder. After less than thirty seconds, one of the women anxiously interrupted the quiet and started talking again. She complained of a hum in her ears and of the troubling sound of the throb of her own heartbeat. Was she afraid of herself? Or of sharing this profoundly intimate moment with others? It seemed to be a common reaction to the silence.

Back in the silence of the tiny village that perched above Lake Lugano, I chopped onions and red peppers to make *peperonata* and polenta for lunch. While concentrating on the slow, regular movement of the knife and the clack, clack as it met the cutting board, I knocked a glass to the floor and it shattered into a hundred tiny slivers. A large shard rocked back and forth as if possessed. I heard, "What did you do that for, silly?" "Huh?" I said. The voice came at me again. "What did you do that for, silly?" Usually a stream of chatter flowed inside my head and went on so long and loud and incessantly that I barely noticed it. But this time I stopped, listened, and called it out.

"I am not silly," I said. "It was an accident. I will pay attention and be more aware next time." The voice inside my head stopped, shocked that I'd noticed, stunned that I dared to defy it and change the recording. This seemingly tiny moment of attention in the silence began a period of great change.

It marked the start of befriending the silence and of being kinder to myself. From that instant, I recognized that particular inner voice as a voice from the past: a relative who put me down as a child, called me silly, and insulted me when I colored outside the lines, spilled a glass of soda pop, or cut my finger. That voice permitted no mistakes. It etched into the grooves of my brain, replayed the same words over and over, and unconsciously built destructive, self-denigrating patterns. Trapped by this voice, I often feared trying new things as a child like diving off a diving board or ballet dancing. But now in the conscious, transformative silence, I confronted it. That moment of awareness broke the bonds of the tyrant past, and a new surge of energy and freedom rushed through me.

All is perfect, I repeated. I am fine. I am growing and improving. My usual subconscious wave of thoughts hesitated, withdrew, and left larger spaces of quiet amidst the stream of mental drivel. Other voices from the past popped in. At a critical time in adolescence, someone close called me a most denigrating name for a woman. I carried the shame of it for years, and part of me felt this must be true since it came from an adult whom I loved. The person despised the feminine, and the comments reflected this. Words can leave wounds that fester and infect us for a lifetime. In the silence, awareness of these wounds rose to the surface and through seeing them in the light of the Swiss Alps and releasing them to evaporate in the dry mountain air, the deep psychic injuries healed. In the silence, I began to know and love myself and ultimately become my own best friend.

Not liking to do things halfway, I set off on a twenty-one day marathon without speaking or eating. I imagined that silence and fasting would propel me into the miracle of no mind where the inner chatter would fall completely silent and I would achieve what I desired most—illumination, nirvana, self-realization. But on the contrary, the more time I spent without food and sound, the louder my mind roared. The exercise seemed futile and pointless until the evening of the twentieth day. I ran a bath, adding myrrh and lavender into the water, and observed the mental diarrhea.

"The Persiano Restaurant serves that yummy tabbouli, falafel, and hummus. It would be soooo good. Then we could go out sailing on the lake and shop at the Manor. Those feathery soft cashmere sweaters. I want two or three. Pastel yellow, blue, pink…" My mind ran on and on like a little child runs from one toy to the next. It played out there in the world while I slowly dropped the essences into the bath. And that's when it struck me. The split. I watched my mind run on and on and yet I didn't get caught up in acting on its whims. I shrugged, observed, and continued to focus on the drops of oil falling into the bath water. I became the witness. Instead of my mind using me as it had done most of my life, it became my instrument.

This marvelous realization changed my world. Until that moment I assumed that I was my mind and my body. During the long fast, my shapely hips disappeared until I required a belt to hold up my pants. This proved I was not my body, because I'd lost much of it in the past three weeks. I swirled inward a step deeper and recognized the mystery of the mind. It lived a turbulent life of its own, but when I identified with the witness, I remained unperturbed by it.

I didn't let it move me, but instead took the time to examine what it wanted to move me to act on. The wiser, higher part of me now took control. Grace had entered into the space in the silence and brought with it the gift of transformation. This step away from my mind into the space of the observer brought a new sense of freedom. From this moment forward I lived from a deeper place, guided more by the soul and less by impulses of the body and mind.

Later, other mysteries unfolded in the light mountain air. While sharpening a pencil or cutting images to create a collage, I heard, or felt rather, the intense thoughts of my friends Marisa in Cannes or Julia in Burgundy. When I called them, they confirmed they had been thinking of me and wanted to ask a question, come visit, had just mailed a letter, or had spoken of me to a friend. Many people report these experiences with the silence. Our thoughts travel faster than the speed of light. They fill the space and are just as real and palpable as words on a computer screen or in a book. Now I think of the silence as a blank page on which to write. Do I fill it with awe and wonder or do I pollute it with base ideas and fear?

Being in the silence makes me conscious of that which is often immaterial and unconscious. But awareness to the shimmering details makes us alert, sensitive instruments that can hear and see far beyond what we limit ourselves to be. I thought back to Karim's words in Egypt as we parted. "You're one of us," he had whispered. Maybe this is what he meant. My body was becoming a finely tuned instrument that picked up the subtle frequencies and shifts of thought, images, and color. I am not special. All humans have the potential to do this, I believe. But I choose to live with the silence and receive its gifts, not fear it. All of my being has become an eye and everything around me is filled with sentient eyes too. The experience draws perception inward to the core to see eye to eye with everything.

This step into a new sensitivity may be sought after, but most people don't realize or may not want the responsibility it brings. What happens when you see and hear thoughts and feelings coming from your friends that they may not even be conscious of? What do you do when you begin to perceive secrets that others aim to hide? This kind of opening presents an opportunity to learn that nothing is hidden. *All* thoughts and actions can be known, including your own. This extra-sensory perception is a gift and a burden given to those who seek to help, and some will also abuse their power.

I felt frightened by the new perceptions. "Love," I heard my heart say. "Love will make it bearable. Love is the answer." But how do you love someone when he stands before you with sex scenes of you clearly unfurling in his mind? How do you love someone who you clearly perceive hates you and wants you to fail when even she isn't fully aware of her own feelings? How do you help someone whose son is gay and invents the story of an imaginary girlfriend for his mother because he's afraid to hurt her feelings? Some people seem to want these gifts without realizing the complexity and responsibility related to them.

Karim, the mystical perfumer in Egypt, had seen into my heart with all of my desires, darkness, pettiness, and fear. I fell in love with him because he understood me. I desired him to be my mate, which he certainly sensed. But in that moment of despair and anxiety, instead of taking advantage of my weakness and need, he respected, loved, and saw me without judgment. He chose to help me and not to use me. His example guided me to find my own inner sacred space and to treat these gifts with the deep respect they deserve. For this I am ever grateful. The soul growth accelerated and required more adaptation in diet and exercise. The next steps required coping with the changes and not settling in to any kind of comfortable routine. Much more mystery and magic would be in store.

Conscious Awareness in Silence

As your meditation practice deepens, bring that sense of being in the present consciously into your daily activities. True meditation takes place not only in the silence of a quiet sacred space, but also when we bring the depth of awareness into every activity in life. Schedule a moment to be silent. Try to make it an hour, half a day, or an entire day. Give yourself permission to simply be. Watch your mind and what it does. Don't read or fill your mind with more clutter during the periods of quiet. If thoughts come, let them pass by like leaves floating down a river. Don't hold on to them. Be present and pay attention to details. If you take a meal in silence, be present to the sensations. Taste, observe, smell, feel, sense, and then go deeper. Later on describe your experiences and your self-observations. Do you enjoy the quiet?

Walking in Natural Silence

If being quiet seems daunting, make a move into nature. We're so often "doing" that we have forgotten how to be. Cultivating a state of receptivity means being attentive, not passive, but holding the space in silent awareness. In the quiet of nature, we may find the pathway to the silent Self more accessible. Nature naturally soothes and cools our taut nerves. On a walk, practice being present with each footstep and breath.

Observe the world both inside and outside of you. How does one reflect the other? Notice a bee dipping into the core of a flower, a black and yellow salamander wriggling across the path, or a goat following you down the mountainside. Pay attention to them, to the glimpse of a hawk in a cypress tree, to the raccoon peering out of a hole in a dead tree trunk. They're subtly present when we pay attention. Each one whispers that splendid life holds mysteries and miracles that can unfold our understanding. The flowers truly do blossom and grow by the power of an unseen force. On your walk, pay attention to the sky. Bring a relaxed focus to your eyes and mind, but don't make it so pinpoint-tight that it strains you. For the first few steps try coordinating your breath with slow, gentle footsteps. Then let go and stroll on at a natural pace through the daisies and lilies.

If you walk in the city, pay attention to the sky. Find an open area where the sky spreads out above. If you will, imagine the sun shining beyond the clouds even if you cannot perceive it. Above the clouds it always shines and it sheds light on all people and things. Its rays dip down and pierce the clouds even in darkest winter and bring invisible vitality. What other natural beauty do you notice? The flash of kindness in a stranger's eye? A blade of grass poking through a crack in the sidewalk? A flower growing on a windowsill? Make a point to look for the beauty.

Tell me what you eat, and I'll tell you who you are.

—JEAN ANTHELME BRILLAT-SAVARIN

Chapter 18
Weeding Some More:
Nourishing Body, Mind, and Soul

Feeding mind, body, and spirit with healthy nourishment can mean the difference between having the energy to grow spiritually and withering. Food is one of the most important elements of physical existence, and learning to consume with moderation and wisdom builds a good foundation for a healthy spiritual life. In France, food is a way of life. What you eat, when, how—it's all elevated to an art so that the body, mind, and soul are nourished.

I loved *dorade, loup,* and other fish with rosé wines from Provence; foie gras served with warm toast and sweet wines like the Monbazillac, Loupiac, or Sauternes; and an occasional steak, but my diet started to naturally evolve. The more I meditated and ventured into my secret garden, the less I liked meat, chicken, turkey, and finally fish, until I slowly stopped eating them all and became vegetarian. This happened in a regular progression, not an overnight cold turkey. It coincides with expansion in human consciousness as we consider all of life worthy of respect. Our diets adapt and we learn about how to cook and consume in a healthier, lighter manner more in tune with nature. It's a process.

Why become a vegetarian? Is it a question of health or philosophy? Well, it's both. I feel healthier and lighter since I stopped eating meats, fish, and poultry. My mind feels calmer. Vegetarian foods provide plenty of variety. I also love animals, but preferably not as meals. Dad hunted and carried home rabbits when I was a child. The same rabbits I'd scampered with in the flowery fields ended up on the dinner plate. It became impossible not to make the connection between the living animals I saw outside and the *lapin à la moutarde* (rabbit in mustard sauce) on my fork.

Friends taunted and provoked. "Oh don't you miss this filet mignon? I feel *so* sorry for you," they'd say. Other friends boasted about their caviar, while I imagined the sturgeon mercilessly gutted and left to die in the sea. My body and psyche felt ready for change. But that didn't mean everyone else had to adapt too. Nor did it mean imposing my views or trying to change others.

Food need not become a dogma or a means of judging the evolution of others. One friend became a vegan. In addition to eating no meat or fish, he ate no eggs, cheese, dairy, or any other animal byproducts. I tried this too and learned that dairy products aren't good for my body. So I cut back some. But on a chilly Riviera evening when I ordered a hot chocolate, the vegan eyed me as if I'd committed a sin. "Hot chocolate contains milk," he snarled. "I'll have a tea with lemon, please." He judged me as immoral. That attitude chilled our relations and sowed division. Best to let everyone make their own decisions based on their needs and conscience and not impose. We all go through periods of learning in different ways and with different timing. Some people may need meat and eggs, and later on my body again needed fish to heal from an illness. Every *body* is different, and our bodies change.

In the big picture, what we consume will influence our state of being and the environment of the world. We know this, but we don't always listen. Many of us are addicted to foods and drinks that hinder our creativity and our ability to relax and be naturally calm, quiet, and healthy. Quitting coffee gave me a ferocious migraine headache. Headaches can represent a symptom of withdrawal from a drug; they are a reaction to addiction as the body works to cleanse itself of something it has learned to live with and come to need. I thought coffee made me more productive, more intensely aware, but instead it clouded my mind and left me agitated and unable to focus, which stifled my creativity. The idea that coffee equaled improved productivity proved an illusion.

Six to eight cups a day of Ethiopian Arabica coffee specially ground at the coffee bean shop in Antibes gave me a great high. The first big cup in the morning made with my expensive espresso machine brought deep pleasure. I loved the ritual—packing the coffee into the machine, flipping the switch, waiting for the pressure to build up with a low hum until the slow, dark liquid dripped thickly into my big cup and the air filled with the rich aroma. Coffee scents wafted up from the corridors in the apartments all around and up from the streets as all of France drank up for a coffee buzz at about the same time. And I loved it. I loved the smell, the ritual of making the espresso and stirring the irregular cubes of raw sugar into porcelain cups with a thin-handled silver spoon. I loved eating a square of dark chocolate at the same time or dipping the point of a croissant into it and savoring the bittersweet combinations. I was in love with a drug and *needed* it to start work in the morning.

But one morning at about ten a.m. after my fourth coffee, I couldn't concentrate on writing. Time to quit. It became my New Year's resolution. So when January first rolled around, I stopped cold. No coffee on this sunny day when the streets were quiet and most of the stores were shut, and people slept in snug under their covers. I awoke early and walked around the Cap d'Antibes, one of my favorite long seaside walks. With only a light breakfast sans coffee and some water, I set out. The sky at that time of year glows clear and brilliant, turning the sea deep blue and the sky almost as rich in color. The sun looks gold and shimmers in the newness of the day.

I walked beneath the lighthouse, down to La Garoupe beach and onto the rocky path (now paved) toward the pirates' path. My head started to ache a little bit. I peeled some Corsican Clementine oranges with the green leaves still attached to the stem and offered one to a woman out walking with her dog. It was too early for most people. New Year's revelers had stayed out late drinking champagne and fêting some notion of starting anew, and lay in bed now nursing hangovers. But I'd had a quiet night with no drinking.

Despite the clean slate, my head ached more with each step. I beelined past the Hôtel du Cap, past the Naval Museum, and down to the jagged white rocks that jut out into the sea.

Down along the roadside where million-dollar villas hang along the seashore and a tiny port harbors wooden fishing boats. The sun continued to rise into the sky and shorten the cool shadows. With each step my head ached and throbbed more. By the time I reached the old stone tower sitting on the water's edge and zeroed in on Juan les Pins, the ache turned into a throbbing, roaring migraine. I hobbled home, holding on to my head with each painful step.

At home I vomited; my face turned an odd shade of yellow as if I had jaundice; and blood spots appeared under my eyes. I drank lots of water and suffered through the night until I finally fell asleep and vowed not to ever go through that again. I've rarely had a cup of coffee since, though I still love the smell. My stomach and liver rejoiced when the toxic bombardment of brown juice stopped. I traded it in for the Swiss-Italian ersatz coffee mixes made with barley, figs, and chicory. This wartime mixture (people said they used it when they had no coffee beans during World War II) didn't have the caffeine punch, but it kept me warm in the mornings and offered a rich, yummy flavor.

Sweet Surrender

I also loved sweets. Eating processed, white sugar took me back to Mom's pies and cookies. I associated them with love and comfort. Without the coffee a new pattern kicked in. Sugar cravings replaced the coffee addiction. At about ten a.m. at low energy tide, I'd run for the chocolate or cookies. They gave a quick pick-me-up too. Then it became a habit. Any time of day when my energy dropped I ran for sweets. I wanted to stay on a sugar high. It felt good. But our bodies go through natural rhythms throughout the day. When I resorted to sugar to give me a boost, I paid the price. It lowered the resistance of my immune system, created an acidic environment where bacteria thrived, and I inevitably got sick. I watched the cycle again and again. Feel low. Eat a lot of sugar to overcome it, and then get a cold, flu, or something more serious.

Finally in observing the pattern I stopped. Observing my own rhythms and habits helped me to become healthy and break the bad habits. Now, fresh and dried fruits replace the white and processed sugars. They give good energy to the body with fewer calories and help to maintain even energy levels. Dreams also brought good information about foods to add to or eliminate from my diet. The messages can be as clear as "No potatoes and no white bread," as one dream announced. I would need to stay in good health for the dark night of the soul on the horizon.

Food for Thought

Foods can affect our thoughts and state of being. Eating healthy, fresh foods in moderate quantities can serve to keep your body in good shape and maintain a calm mind. Take a few minutes to reflect on your diet. You may want to keep a list of your food intake for a week or a month to observe your habits. Habits like expensive coffee or chocolates may not only be costly to your pocketbook, but they may also cost you in health and peace of mind.

Enter into your secret garden space, and in the quiet, invite in your inner guidance. Gently reflect on your relationship to food. What does it mean to nourish your body? Do you pay proper attention to this vital act of affirming life? Do you feel a sense of gratitude for your meals? Do you yearn for home-cooked food? Is there something you would like to change in your eating? Instead of watching TV at mealtime, turn your meals into rituals that nourish your body, mind, and soul by adding a candle or flowers to the table.

Newspapers, books, TV, and company we spend time with provide another form of food for the soul. If the mind feeds on criticism, violence, and bad news, then these will influence our thoughts and actions during the day. Spending a week without reading opened my eyes to the way my mind devoured the words and works of others—so much so that I couldn't hear my own thoughts. Over the next days, consider the ways you nourish yourself on all levels. What do you feed your mind? How might you give it nourishment that will uplift you? What do you do to nourish your soul? Do you take walks in nature, meditate, spend time in a group of spiritual-minded friends? Would you like to change anything?

In the time of darkness we have never been closer to the light.

—MEISTER ECKHART

Chapter 19

Death and Dark Nights in the Garden: Reaching Spiritual Maturity

Sooner or later you may find yourself in a dark night where it seems that all of the light suddenly vanishes. An illness arrives. A loved one dies. A marriage falls apart and faith disappears. Doubts creep in, and it's easy to lose hope and wonder, "Why bother cultivating a spiritual life when it affords no assurance that all will work out?" When the dark night arrives it's like the arrival of winter in the secret garden. But even in the dark chill, things continue to grow silently out of sight.

When death crept into my secret garden, it challenged my spiritual maturity. I assumed that if I cultivated my inner life and deepened my relationship with the Divine, the path would be always happy and carefree. If I did all of the right things—listened to my inner gardener, ate properly, exercised, followed my conscience in making decisions—then I would be free of illness and catastrophe, I thought. All of life would be a constant joy and run smoothly. Spiritual practice must be like an insurance policy, right? my mind reasoned in a stock-exchange way. If I meditate, fast, eat right, etc., then I will receive a life without any problems. This seemed logical, a fair trade, a proper exchange. But logic and exchange are not the currency of the soul.

My dear friend and housemate, Giovanni, cultivated a secret garden too. We shared meals and friends, walks and talks, meditations, parties, and a trip to an ashram and a hugging saint. I couldn't make sense of a dream that warned me to be supportive of Gio, but to keep an emotional distance. Burdened by huge financial obligations and an unfair separation from his daughters, he slumped under the weight of despair. But he loved salsa and he'd started to dance regularly. On this particular Saturday night he invited me along. He flirted with women, shook his cute Swiss-Italian butt, and made us laugh with his dark humor. The scene marked a sign of hope that the heavy pall of depression hanging over the house for months would soon vanish.

I left him on the dance floor and drove home to a deep and restful sleep. Then a shot rang out at three a.m. The explosion rattled the windows and cut through the deep silence of the night. I lay frozen in bed, afraid to move. I lived in an upstairs apartment in the house and knew immediately that a living nightmare was unfolding. The sound of footsteps and low voices echoed outdoors. Was it a murder? Terror paralyzed me until I recognized the voice of Gio's father along with his stepmother. They lived in the house next door. They pounded on the door downstairs, and when no one responded they opened it with a spare key. A terrible scream broke the silence. In a few minutes his dad stood at my door, pale as the moon.

"It's Gio," he said. "He's shot."

My mind couldn't comprehend it. The words didn't translate into any sort of reality that made sense. "Call an ambulance!" I said, and I began to run down the stairs before Gio's dad grabbed me.

"No," he said. "Stay here." And then through silent tears: "He left some notes."

The shock of his suicide acted like an earthquake in my world. What happened?! I imagined that beautiful, sensitive man in a pool of blood. How could he have left his precious life and his lovely children? I wept.

Why bother to make all the efforts to cultivate this sacred inner place as we had both been doing if tragedies continue to strike? Why cultivate a better life and work with guiding values if they will not protect from pain? These thoughts whirred through my mind as friends called to ask about Gio and express their frustration at not having been able to help. Many felt guilty. In the aftermath and the silence of the big house we had shared, I felt Gio's presence and his regret. Nothing had been solved by his choice. And I missed him terribly. His children missed him too, and I felt an empty hole in my heart.

In that time of transition and deep questioning, I reread the story of Rama. Rama, a beautiful, powerful, and sweet Indian avatar, fought against the ten-headed demon, Ravana, who abducted his wife, Sita. Rama sought to protect his future kingdom through virtue and right action. He grew up in peace and wealth; yet on the day of his coronation he became an exile from his own kingdom and was sent to live in the forest for seven years for no fault of his own.

He walked peacefully away from the luxury of jewels and silks and wore matted hair and simple clothes into the forest. The avatar eventually conquered Ravana and reunited with his wife, the kidnapped Sita. At the end of his exile he returned to his kingdom, where under his rule even the gods envied men and women for their paradisaical lives. I loved the beautiful story of Rama's kingdom and imagined a paradise on Earth. How beautiful to have lived under his rule, I thought. But in the end even Rama suffered decline and left his physical body.

In the secret garden, decline and death of the body and the physical realm are a natural part of life. In a new phase of spiritual maturity and growth, I realized that no amount of prayer, meditation, or devotion would prevent pain, suffering, or mortality. Though we deny it, illness, decline, and decay remain part of the natural ebb and flow. Imagine a world where nobody died? Overpopulation would choke out any hope for a quality life. In the garden, decaying compost acts as fertilizer to the life of the flower or fruit that follows. Material forms change, but cultivating the connection with the Divine creates a foundation, a solid ground to stand firm on when things seem to fall apart all around.

I don't know why Giovanni chose to commit such an act of self-destruction. He faced many challenges: threats of loss of his home, a deepening custody battle for the kids, financial strains, and the untimely death of his mother. But no real explanation seems to account for the ultimate tragedy. The grief that surrounded his demise led some friends who traveled with us to India to question the purpose of maintaining a spiritual practice at all. Some of them lost faith in the Divine. If spiritual practice doesn't protect against pain and shore us up against death, then why bother, some asked and turned bitter. Some people even turned away from their spiritual practice. Pondering in silence, I discovered that despite deep grief and sadness, my heart remained attached to the wise inner gardener and the divine source of all life. My mind focused on the still waters beneath the surface of the physical world and not on the rough waves at the top.

When I scuba-dived deep beneath the Mediterranean, the rough weather could not move me. The currents rushed fast and furious near the surface by the boat, but deep below the sea, grass danced gently and the waves could not buffet me much. The same happened in the storms of life. If I stayed deep inside, tried to help distraught friends with encouraging words, and watched the tears flow during moments of meditation, the calm reigned. In a little while, acceptance arrived and the storms passed. Calm eventually returned to the surface too and life continued. The secret garden reveals that this is the way of nature in its eternal cycle of birth, life, and death. All physical things pass. But the spirit never dies.

Months later, I watched orange-robed monks express this message of the transitory and ephemeral nature of life through art. They tapped metal cones of bright sand into a design that became an exquisite and intricate sand mandala at the Manor department store in downtown Lugano. For a week they sat on a square wooden pedestal that resembled a large shelf among the stationery, Swiss milk chocolate, and stuffed dairy cows sold to tourists. It looked as if anyone might buy one of the smiling, calm Buddhist monks and take him home to put on their shelf.

As their work continued, grain by grain, a circle formed inside a square until a delicate, ephemeral healing mandala for the goddess Tara appeared beneath their brown hands. So careful and conscientious, they drew out the design and filled it in—tap, tap, tap—while consumers dawdled and sought bliss in candy and clothes. On Saturday after a consecration with mantras and chants, a ritual whisk of the brush turned the vibrant yellow, green, red, and blue mandala into a pile of gray.

The entire, perfectly organized work of art transformed into a dull, shapeless mass of sand. Through a week of intensive work, chanting, and silence, they revealed the process of life as it became a mandala. It organized into an intricate form, which lived a short life and then experienced dissolution. Their final ritual confirmed the life cycle. They released the mandala sands in a nearby river, where they washed toward the sea as a reminder of our own journey toward the vast ocean of consciousness.

Rather than find my faith shaken by Gio's suicide, in the end I accepted the divine play and understood that mysteries and reasons exist far beyond my small view of the world. At the same time, the inner waters had been tested and the power of my inner life stood firm and affirmed, like a giant oak tree. Light returned and the blossoms that had begun to wither in the darkness once again opened.

So the answer to my question about whether cultivating a spiritual life will protect from pain remains twofold. No, cultivating a secret garden will not protect from life's difficulties. Challenges will continue to arise. Life as long as we live will be filled with worries and problems. And yes, if we remain focused inward and continue to cultivate the secret garden, we will find protection and refuge from mental madness and despair. The pain fades more quickly as peace and joy quickly take the place of suffering. Moments of inner reflection offer quiet refuge from the storm and allow for solutions to arise and periods of calm to prevail. Serenity, even through life's ups and downs, becomes the nature of the well-tended inner place of the soul.

This gentle acceptance of life's troubles signaled a move into spiritual maturity and spiritual practices like meditation and chanting provided tools for coping. Holding a spiritual perspective affords a view and Self-confidence that some-one who focuses solely on the material world is not open to receive. It provides a profound sense of the mysterious and incomprehensible movements of life and a way to feel at one with it and accept. For me it signaled a move into a deep connection with the mysteries of the Divine Mother as she began to appear and light the path.

Peace or Pieces in the Garden

In periods of challenge and crisis, if we allow our-selves to get caught up in the material madness of life, then making sense of events escapes us. Fear takes over as we identify ourselves and others as the body only. By retreating into the secret garden and looking from the spiritual perspective, we may find it easier to accept that an invisible hand works from a higher place and in a way that we cannot possibly fathom with our limited abilities.

A friend injured in a serious car accident as a teen-ager found himself fully healed from the physical injuries. The arm that doctors had intended to amputate healed and he came out determined and strongminded. Yet the question "Why me?" paralyzed him. He put his life on hold for twenty years to look for the response to a question that no one could answer. His entire identity revolved around being the victim of a car accident and he announced this to most any new acquaintance in their first five minutes of meeting. If he had been able to shift his perception and accept the event as a way to learn essential life lessons and develop his courage and tenacity, it would have completely transformed him.

Sometimes the practice of surrender or acceptance is the way to find true peace of mind. In the Garden of Gethsemane, Jesus prayed intensely for a change in what he foresaw coming—and added, "Your will, not mine." He prayed for a change, but he also accepted the outcome. In the silence of your secret garden, do you have "whys" that haunt you and block your path? Can you surrender them at the feet of your wise soul-Self or your image of the Divine and let them go? Sometimes these questions hold us in a state of paralysis as we await answers that we must instead live into. What difficult situations and problems are you ready to surrender now? If you're ready, enter into the core of your sacred, secret garden with your unanswered questions. Put them in a letter or a package for your wise inner gardener and surrender them to her. Let her pass them on to a higher place where all merges in peace and bliss. Sometimes unexpected blessings and even answers arrive to help us to understand some of life's mysteries.

Mourning Something Lost

Rituals help us to heal. They help us to acknowledge the changes in life, bring to light and resolve buried feelings that may accompany the death of a loved one, and allow them to heal. This is a good time to take a moment to think of a loss that you mourn but have not fully acknowledged. It may relate to a relationship, a possession, a job, a person, or something else. Reflect on it a moment. You may want to write about this or share it with a friend. Make a symbol of what you've lost on a piece of paper or visualize it in your heart. Let your feelings well up and accompany the symbol. Light a candle for it, mourn it, and then let it dissolve into the Divine Light.

Chapter 20

Embracing Divine
Feminine Nature

All along this path, the feminine aspect of God slowly drew
me in and revealed the inner strength of the feminine ways
of intuition, dreams, and soulful insights. On the way up to
the Madonna del Sasso, a sixteenth-century monastery above
Locarno, Switzerland, the cobblestone path steepened and
my breath grew heavy. Hidden in a passage by the stone
archway, a larger-than-life Mother Mary dressed in a flowing gown stood adorned with stars. She perched on top of
a vicious red dragon. In most Catholic churches and cathe-
drals, Mary resembles a docile, meek woman—inoffensive,
unobtrusive, and lovely. But here she represented a powerful

and magnificent goddess with divine powers that vanquish the dark forces. She towered above the path, erect and confident; her robe flowed behind her as if she walked into a gust of wind.

The dragon's jagged teeth and horned tail seemed bent on destruction, but Mary's feet were planted firmly on it and the dragon writhed beneath her, unable to escape; her face remained confident, peaceful, and unruffled. She greeted me from the arched threshold by the chapel and filled me with a sense of encouragement and power. Her feminine powers conquered the demonic shadows and brought them into balance with the masculine. Under her gentle gaze, the intuitive silence, receptivity, the nurturing of nature, and the deep connection with the Divine prevailed.

From the beginning of this journey, the Mother yearned for expression, but a stalker sought to kill her presence. The Divine Feminine helped me to leave behind the business role, find the spiritual baby on the ocean floor, and bring it to the surface. She appeared in the form of a guide glowing with light and helped me to reunite the feminine pieces of myself like Isis reunited the pieces of Osiris. But the more I felt comfortable with her presence and her whispering of deep intuition, the more the stalker lurked and threatened to attack. This stalker represented an aspect of my ego that felt angry at taking a seat behind her growing presence.

As a child when I began to think things were going well, when my writing flowed and I felt happy and carefree, this terrifying dream would arise:

I'm outdoors at night alone. A shadow man approaches me and he is as dark as the darkness. I walk fast through the dewy grass and my bare legs grow damp and chilled. The man approaches, looms closer and faster, bearing down on me. A knife the size of a man's forearm, steely and honed, slashes at me. I run and try to scream, but no sound emerges. The blocked sound sends me into panic and despair. Screamless, voiceless, I'm doomed to receive the stalker's blows.

For years I woke up trembling from the horror of having no voice and seeing the feminine side of me killed off in dreams in the dark night. As an adult when I began to feel comfortable and fully embrace the inner explorations, the stalker showed up in my secret garden ready to kill off the progress. He appeared in my waking life as a mentor whom I asked to help me grow as a writer and find my voice. Because he was a respected author who won awards and international acclaim, I appealed to him for guidance in my writing career. He read some of my work and suggested that I stick to writing letters to friends rather than pursue my dreams of publishing articles, essays, and books. Through him I became aware of the stalker archetype in my psyche, and once I recognized it, I booted the misogynist author out of my life.

The woman-hating stalker inside destroys. It lived in me as the hard, driven, overly rational, aggressive part of me personified in the businesswoman who refused to acknowledge, respect, and give voice to the feminine qualities. But as a spiritual seeker, the stalker had to die to leave space for the Divine Feminine and allow her to come into balance with the Divine Masculine.

Ultimately the Divine Mother gave me the courage needed to kill the female-hating demon within that tried to strangle the growth of love for her and the gifts of intuition she gave. Symbols of the Mother stood in many shrines along the paths and roads in Switzerland, Italy, and France. Though I'm not Catholic, these feminine images of the spiritual force moved deep into my psyche and provided nourishment during the long dark nights of bitter cold and silence. They infused a sense of confidence that I too, with the help of the Divine Feminine, would conquer my inner demon and unify the masculine with the feminine.

In the business world I adopted male attitudes and suppressed my feminine, intuitive side to survive. Little by little the masculine qualities of assertiveness, drive, bravery, and tenacity took over and I transformed into an "honorary man" to fit into the masculine-minded business world. My instincts and intuitions whispered, "There's something more." But a thick, hard shell grew up around my heart. The shell provided protection in a harsh environment, but it also numbed me and brought my spirit to shrivel. The wiser part of me whispered, "It's time to change." It encouraged me to start this journey, embrace and marry my feminine side, and find balance.

A demon stood in the way. He haunted me from within, called my feminine side low, weak, and base. "As a woman, you carry the burden of the original sin," that demon said. "You have to give birth as a curse, not a miracle." He loomed large and heavy as he denigrated even the most exquisite expressions of feminine beauty and power. But quietly and at a regular pace the feminine ways of dreams, symbols, rituals, and intuition took root and grew like a waxing moon to force him out.

The intuitive side grew strong and revealed the final battle over the demon in a terrifying dream early one crisp, cold, Alpine morning.

I arrest a demon man, ugly and insidious. He hates and pursues me and intends to injure and destroy me. But like Mother Mary on the dragon, I stand on top of the man, lean down and strangle him until his writhing body becomes limp and lifeless. All of this time I sing a sweet melody and feel soft, peaceful, and yet very powerful. There's no feeling of hatred or violence. I chant, "Mother oh Mother. Mother oh Mother. Satham, Shivam, Sundarum, Shivoham, Shivoham. All is Love. All is One." The power comes through me, through my voice and sound.

I awoke with my heart hammering wildly, shocked that I had just killed someone in my dream. I practice nonviolence to the point of capturing spiders and ants that slip indoors, carefully putting them out on the grass rather than killing them. The potency of this scene astounded me. But dream images often are not what they seem. I'd killed a stalker. He represented a hateful demon within me who despised all things feminine, considering them weak. He hated the female body and soft, feminine qualities. He despised my voice and my song.

I'd learned some of the words in India. "Satham, Shivam, Sundarum" means truth, goodness, and beauty in Sanskrit. *Shivoham* is the word that the enlightened ones pronounce when they merge fully with the Divine. The song came together as a feminine battle cry, sung from a peaceful, powerful heart, the heart of the Mother. She, in her many forms, took root in my heart and gave me the strength to value and perceive the power of compassion, cooperation, kindness, and selfless love.

In Antibes the Mother perched in the Chapel at La Garoupe next to the lighthouse on the Cap where families of fishermen brought gifts and prayers to protect their loved ones at sea. The walls of the cool Romanesque chapel were adorned with paintings, photos, and letters of gratitude from hundreds of years ago to recent times. The Mother dressed in gold, glimmering with her babe in arms, stood strong as the protector, the nurturer, the one who gives life. In June, the fishermen bring her out on a pedestal and carry her down the path of the cross in a long procession, past the sea front, past the tourists in bikinis, and bring her to the main cathedral. Her presence blesses the surroundings with the feminine principle of love.

In the Camargue I saw her at Saintes Maries de la Mer, where the French recount the legend that the three Marys arrived from Jerusalem after the slaying of Jesus. In the cathedral, below the main floor, Sarah of Kali stood, black as ebony, dressed in gowns of cloth. I waited in line, crowded together with pilgrims in the dark space where candles burned and turned the low ceiling of the vaulted room black. The air became hot and heavy, and there was little space to maneuver. Roma gypsies, who some believe came from India eons ago, adore Sarah. Each year they migrate here in flocks, like the thousands of pink flamingos that feed in the marsh a kilometer away. The Roma carry Sarah out of the church and into the sea in a ritual baptism.

In India I met Kali. She wore a necklace of human heads. At first glimpse both the black Sarah and Kali sent shivers through me. But they represent the natural yet mystical processes of life. Kali does not take human heads out of malice. She represents the movement of physical time, that aspect of life from which nobody can escape. Mother Kali's name comes from the feminine form of the Sanskrit word *kala*, which means time. Time is Kali's power to destroy, for nothing can escape her constant movement forward.

For much of my existence, I'd imagined that life could be lived in boxes. I tried to categorize people, experiences, and things in pigeonholes and imagined rows and rows of vertical and horizontal boxes. My left-brained, reasoning mind liked this neat, tidy way of functioning. A thing is either good or bad. It is black or white. But the feminine principle grasps the subtleties and complexities of life and accepts its shifting nature. It focuses on the process, while the male side aims for the result. An event may be good for me and bad for someone else. It admits the gray areas, that relationships, people, and things constantly shift, and wax and wane like the moon. It feels the nuances of thought and relies on the wisdom heart and deeper perception to assess a situation.

It *knows* even before understanding why. Flashes arrive in images and sensations. A deep level of knowing strikes a chord of truth that resonates throughout one's being. This is the feminine principle—airy, light, shifting, subtle, and heartfelt. It works best when balanced with the masculine—reason, concrete, practical, action. The Mother integrates and unifies. She seeks the welfare of many and makes sacrifices to see that others are served and healed. Think of Mother Teresa, who devoted her life to giving succor to the most destitute and outcast. Her strength became apparent when I heard from friends who traveled to Calcutta to work in her foundation. Some left after only two or three days, unable to bear the sight of the pain and sickness of the lepers and the orphaned children. Mortality appeared cruel and unusual in my masculine world, but it fit in perfect harmony with Mother Nature as I watched the seasons shift through spring, summer, fall, and back to the silence of winter. The Mother whispered that being creative and alive feels good and joyful. But blocking creativity will destroy. Change, the Mother reminds us, is natural. Embrace it.

Embracing the Mother

Is there an image of the Divine Mother that appeals to you? It may be your physical mother, the inner gardener and guide who lives within you, an image of a deity, or a symbol that represents the feminine principle. For many of us, our grandmothers embodied feminine ideals. Put the image on your altar or in your sacred space. Breathe and let your body relax. Let your mind follow the breath. When you're ready, move deep into your sacred space. Take this image of the feminine and in your imagination hold it to your heart. Let it fill you. Appreciate and love the soft sweetness and the nurturing your Mother brings. When you're ready, return to the world knowing that the sacred feminine is always there to nurture and guide you when you need it.

Balancing the Feminine and Masculine

Giving voice to the feminine, spontaneous, playful side of the psyche nurtures a healthy, happy soul. The demon stalker turned up in dreams to ravage my psyche and threaten my spiritual baby, but to protect myself I faced him and sang out a clear, pure song that annihilated his deadly influence. Music, singing, dance, playing an instrument, writing, doing art, and expressing your creative voice in whatever way feels right for you destroys the killjoy demon stalker within and gives expression to your soul-Self. The soul-Self represents the feminine aspect of the Divine. Expressing it will aid in bringing a balance with the masculine side of the Divine. Some soulful feminine qualities may include openness to intuition, softness, nurturing, and attention to insights, while some masculine qualities might include reasoning, putting things into action, and will. How can you work to promote an inner marriage between the two so that they live in harmony as one?

Part Four

Harvesting the Joy

The tree gives shade and fruits to one and all
without distinction for class, color, creed, or
whether those benefiting are good or bad.

Seen through the eyes of love, all beings are beautiful, all acts are dedicated, and the world is one vast family.

—SAI BABA

Chapter 21

Reaping the Harvest: Recognizing the Divine in All

In the secret garden the seeds planted months and even years ago now grow into huge trees; vineyards fill with sweet grapes ready to harvest; flowers grow abundantly. This beautiful inner landscape is the result of strenuous work both inside by tending thoughts and also in daily activities. Thoughts, words, and actions align to serve, share good energy, and make the world a better place. In the beginning the pieces of oneself are spread out and cut off from each other. Through regular tending and concentrated effort, the different levels of the mind begin to merge into one. Instead of sleeping on a decision to gain insights, the intuitive information comes in readily and easily. The masculine and feminine marry at the altar of the Divine in peaceful unity. It's time to reap the harvest of a peaceful and harmonious life.

The mind seeks out division between good and evil, love and hate, sacred and profane. It creates an either/or world. But the deeper I dived, the higher I climbed, and the more that I used my heart, the more I realized that this divided view of reality was unreliable. A hawk screeched its piercing cry and dived for a rabbit. If the hawk missed, it might die of hunger. If it succeeded, then the rabbit would die. Did this make the beautiful red-shouldered hawk evil to kill its prey? I felt perplexed. I may not need meat for lunch, but the hawk's nature requires it to eat meat to survive. In my limited view, I judged. But what a useless waste of energy! I could no more judge the rightness of a hawk's kill than of my neighbor's purchase of a Range Rover. While eating rabbits and buying a Rover wouldn't be right for me, who could see all of the reasons and events that led to the action for another? Who could know the depth of it and all of the cause and effect that went before?

Late into nights, I pondered over duality and the nature of life. If there were no darkness, we could not know light. Without pain and anxiety, we would not know the nature of peace. Without sadness it's impossible to know the existence of happiness. Without hate, how could we recognize love? Through the opposites, we become conscious of the multifaceted nature of life. Beauty lies in contrast. Divinity lies in bridging the opposites. The teacher at the ashram in India taught the practice of seeing all as God. See all as good, he said. "Think good, see good, be good, do good." This is a way to unite the opposites. Through this practice, wisdom arises and the mind begins to explore the nature of goodness and what it truly means. Very often goodness relies on perspective. Think of the hawk again. From the hawk's perspective, it's good to catch the rabbit. But from the rabbit's perspective, it's good to escape being eaten. From a higher, divine perspective where the essence of the rabbit and hawk are the same, there is no good or bad; there's simply a play of life as it unfolds.

Krishna, in his enlightening discourse to Arjuna in the *Bhagavad Gita*, gives some insight to this higher perspective. When the story begins, Krishna and Arjuna drive in a chariot across the battlefield just before the fight. Arjuna sees many people he once called friends and mentors on the opposing side and loses heart. He says to Krishna that he cannot slay them, that his actions would be judged as bad. But Krishna sees from the perspective of divinity. These people are destined to die today, he says. You can be a part of this and go down in history as a great warrior, accepting to do what you have been trained for your whole life. Or you can turn away and go down in history as a coward. He goes on to say that the body dies. That's a fact of life. But the essence that animates the body is eternal, unchanging bliss.

Neither the one who slays nor the one who imagines being slain perceives Reality. "For the soul there is neither birth nor death," he says. "The soul is not born and therefore never dies." With these words we're moved into the deepest recognition of our self as divine. That recognition completely shifts the ways we relate to the world. It recognizes that all things physical are transitory. All relationships to the body will pass, but the essence that animates and illuminates it remains untouched and immortal. "I am not the body, for the body will be changed like an old dress. I am not the mind, because the mind too will flicker and fade. I am atman, the eternal, unchanging Self," the inner gardener whispers.

At this level of acceptance, wisdom, and surrender in the secret garden, everything thrives. Harmony prevails and fruits begin to ripen. It's sometimes easiest and safest to contemplate this and experiment with it inside the walls of your secret garden.

Touching the Immortal Self

A part of experiencing unity and oneness comes through intellectual learning about the concept. But the heart can open to a direct and very real experience of it. Over time through meditation and a gentle opening to life, the veil of separation falls. Through opening up and loving all of humanity, that connection to others expands. If you'd like, explore what it means to see all as one. You may do this by considering everyone you meet as divine. How will you speak to the God in front of you in the form of the cashier or the person who just insulted you? How will you accept and love that person? Through this practice, you will begin to experience yourself as Divine. You'll see your deep capacity to love and accept. This experience will be a gift that you give to those around you. It will be transformative for both you and those you meet.

Unity Principle—Getting Head, Heart, and Hands Working Together

See good, do good, be good is one of the best spiritual practices to promote both inner and outer unity. It gets the mind, heart, and hands all working in the same, unified direction. This powerful practice requires careful attention to the words we speak. It means making a commitment to keep our word, and consciously looking for the good, the God, in all. This week pay attention to how you see, what you say, and what you do. Do you think one thing, say another, and do yet another? There is great power in paying attention and getting oneself aligned with the wisdom heart and acting from the deepest, best impulses. What commitment will you make to align thoughts, words, and actions?

One day it was suddenly revealed to me that everything
is Pure Spirit ... Whatever I saw I worshiped.

—RAMAKRISHNA

Chapter 22

Secret Garden Walls Fall

In the beginning a secret garden needs walls to protect the delicate seedlings trying to grow. But once they've taken root and grown into a beautiful landscape, why not let the walls down—at least some of the time? Invite in friends. Share the growth and beauty with family. Dare to reveal a little of your spiritual self to colleagues. Opening the gate to others and even tearing down walls mark big steps toward integration.

Back in Switzerland on a hike above a little village called Sagno, where white marble angels bigger than life adorned the altar of a small Catholic church, I strolled along the path alone, in silence. An Alpine bird sang out the sweetest, most beautiful song. I stopped, closed my eyes to listen, and opened my heart. Relaxed in concentrated love for the tiny creature perched high and invisible in the branches, the warbling song connected us.

Love of the bird and its music expanded my heart until, eyes closed, I felt its tiny heart beating. Its heart became my heart. In silent reverence, we merged into one. A mystical union occurred beyond my will or understanding. It felt sublime, blissful, quiet.

When my mind kicked in and started to recognize the merging, it panicked and jerked me back into separation. The bird must have felt it too, because it flew away startled at the same instant. "Wait a minute," my mind protested. "I am separate. I am not a bird. You know it's not possible to feel a bird's heart." My head felt rattled by the experience of expansion and argued for separation, for keeping up the boundaries and fences. But my heart knew the experience was more real than any of the walls I'd put up. I loved animals. I loved the bird. Without thinking or forcing, the love had made us one.

Similar incidents began to happen with people. In Antibes, some friends arrived and introduced me to a man from London. When we shook hands, I grasped my heart and felt deep pain. I'd felt fine and content until this encounter. But my heart ached and shattered like breaking glass. I wanted to cry, but didn't know why. The feeling lingered as we all went for a drink at a small café. Then I overheard the young man say that his girlfriend had recently broken up with him and that he felt overwhelming sadness. My heart felt his hurting heart. What was happening to me?

Later a friend called to talk. During the conversation, I felt like I was suffocating and I struggled to breathe. I needed air. Ten minutes later my friend said, "I feel like I'm suffocating." I knew she did. I felt it too. I felt it as if we were one and the same. These empathic experiences defy the rational, logical way of thinking about life, which says, *This is me. This is mine. This is where I start and you stop.* Barriers between you and me fall and we literally come to understand that we "do unto others" because one's self and the other are one and the same. In this expansive place, hearts and thoughts merge.

On another occasion, walking down a narrow street in a Swiss village, I felt struck by fear. The sky glowed a crystalline light blue; the sun shimmered on the chestnut trees; and the air smelled pure. All seemed peaceful, yet I clutched my heart and wondered what the feeling meant. Looking around, there seemed to be no apparent danger. The fear came from outside. It belonged to someone else. Around the bend, I saw a woman with her tiny lap dog walking up the road. The fear emanated from her in a cloud that filled a huge radius. Her dog had bitten me once and I now realized she communicated her fear to it, which made it aggressive. The two of them lived in perpetual terror. That strong feeling of fear came from her!

Disassociated fear again floated in the air during my meditations in the Swiss Alps on September 10th, 2001. It hung in the air like a cloud of dread as if the whole world knew of the looming September 11th catastrophe and the change it would wreak on the world. When a friend called to announce the news of the collapse of the Twin Towers a day later, I knew the fear had come from the many people who had unconsciously sensed the arrival of the dreadful event on the eve of the disaster. We are all connected, and that connection transcends time and space as well as levels of awareness.

In 1966 a similar tragedy occurred that showed our profound connection and how we often know of events before they happen. At Aberfan, Wales, torrential rains created a mudslide from the coal waste in the mining village, killing many people. Before the disaster several people reported dreams and premonitions of it. A researcher interviewed villagers after the fact and recorded their experiences. No fewer than sixty people had dreamed of or sensed dread of the event before it happened. A mother reported that her ten-year-old daughter woke up the day before and said she dreamed she wanted to go to school but there was no school. Something black covered it. The next day the slide wiped out the school, and many schoolchildren, including the dreamer, perished. Imagine if someone would have paid attention to the dreams and premonitions!

Animals often foreshadow and know of coming events, too. Elephants in Sri Lanka escaped the disastrous tsunami by moving to high ground many hours before the waves hit. Some part of us is also alerted to danger and knows to move if we pay attention and listen. It also knows when all feels right and when to freely reach out and help.

As time passes, not only feelings but thoughts too become more apparent. They arrive like kind letters from the post office or like punches from people with negative intentions. Like radio waves that carry words through the air, if your receiver is on and tuned to the frequency, the waves can be deciphered and words become clear. Sensitivity to thoughts functions in a similar way. In my kitchen, while cooking, when my mind is clear, I sometimes hear friends who need help, and I call or send loving thoughts. The unkind thoughts of people who wish ill arrive, too. They also need loving prayers. In the silence, nothing remains hidden. Motives arise, feelings emerge and become known like invisible ink on a piece of paper. By brushing the paper with the light of love, certain images and intents become clear.

Every thought, word, and deed counts. I had heard this and shrugged before, but now the meaning translated into experience and understanding. By the sea, a circle of light appeared around a seagull. The auras appeared around other birds also as they flew through the sky. When two flew close together, I imagined the two auras that encircled them separately would simply overlap and be connected at the edges, but still maintain two separate and distinct circles. Instead they merged and made one larger circle. When a flock flew together, the circle enlarged even more to create a bigger energy field. The same happens around people as well. The energy we carry influences others. We are not separate, but a collective whole. Our state of being interacts with others in subtle and powerful ways. The essence that fills all of us, all animals, all of life and inert things, vibrates with the Divine. Through love, we can know the hearts of all.

Our moods, intentions, feelings, and thoughts communicate subtly. In Egypt, long before I imagined any of these experiences possible, Karim, the perfumer in Cairo, read my heart. "You live in France," he said. "You have no children and you are going through a period of transition." He had introduced me to the thoughts, stories, and feelings that I wore like a perfume and he possessed the ability to sense and interpret them. The perfumer's expressions of kindness and his unusual gift of seeing into hearts added a new dimension to my garden. The deeper step into oneness with all people and things opened the doors to my heart. The heart marks that critical point of balance between the material and spiritual worlds, between reason and intuition. When it opens and the energy of love flows through, unhindered life becomes a joy.

Breaking Down Barriers

If you wish to let the barriers around your secret garden expand, begin working with the light meditation. You may wish to sit in front of a candle and watch the flame. When you're ready, close your eyes and imagine the flame inside of your heart. From your heart let it fill your entire body limb to limb, up into your head, your eyes, your mouth and ears. Ask the light to purify your thoughts and the words that come from your mouth. Ask it to let you hear, see, and speak good things. Let the light continue to fill all of your being. Bring the focus to your heart and let the rays of light shine out. As you visualize the light expanding from your heart and emanating from you, imagine that it permeates those closest to you—your mate, friends, and family. Expand it to include neighbors, your whole town or city. Let it expand out toward strangers, and finally let it fill those you resist, those you may condemn, and those you imagine to be enemies until it fills the entire world. Linger in this expanded sense of light.

When you're ready, slowly return to your body and heart. Leave the flame of light burning brightly in the center of your heart. When you go through the days, focus on the light, that spark of love that ignites each heart and sparkles in the eyes of the people who stand before you day in and day out. Relate to others with compassion and watch how both you and they transform. Search for the good and the elevated in the hearts and lives of those around you. Integrate this as a conscious, constant practice.

Merging with the Inner Gardener

For a portion of the journey, the higher self—the one I call the wise, inner gardener—appears as separate. But the deeper we move into the heart of the secret garden, the more we merge with her until there is no longer any separation at all. The two aspects of our Self—one that is alert to the material world, and the other, which appears to guide us from an elevated, light place—become one. We no longer need to go to sleep to dream and receive her messages. Those messages and images arrive at any time of day and we welcome them as gifts. The two wills and desires—those of the outer self, the personality; and the soul-Self—merge into one cohesive and coherent whole. This unity within one's self marks a big leap toward wholeness and harmony with the world.

As you work through and tend the inner spaces in your beautiful, sacred garden of the spirit, have you noticed a merging between these two aspects of yourself? How does this feel? If you still struggle with believing that you hold this wisdom in your depths and doubt that you are a spark of the Divine, take a moment to enter deep within your sacred garden and meditate on the wise gardener who helps you tend to the spiritual. Can you imagine the two of you merging into one? Take a moment to explore this in writing or through some form of artistic expression.

Pilgrimage—a journey, especially a long one
made as an act of devotion to some sacred place.
—WEBSTER'S DICTIONARY

Chapter 23

Coming Home

In Europe, many friends set out on pilgrimages from Geneva, Lyon, or Biarritz across France and on to the Cathedral of Santiago of Compostela in Spain. The long journey takes them across the Pyrenees mountains and carries them through long passages of solitude and tiny villages with barely a hostel or café. At the end of the trail, hundreds of miles and many days away, is the sea and the cathedral containing the relics of St. James. More than the destination, the journey becomes a joy of discovery. Travelers walk long days and sleep in monasteries or hostels by night. They give themselves the gift of time to reflect and connect with other seekers who also seek the sacred. The journey takes them out of their ordinary life of offices, children, families, and comforts, into the world of the spirit.

A friend, Lucina, walked alone on the route to Santiago for months. One day in the fall after a period of seeing no one for miles, her loneliness shifted. "I felt a benevolent presence walking with me," she said. Her eyes turned dreamy and her voice softened as she spoke. "I thought of the millions of pilgrims who walked this road before me. I knew I wasn't alone." Despite rain, uncertain lodging, and losing her way, Lucina said someone always showed up at the right time to offer assistance or point the way. She felt comforted and aided by the encouraging presence of other pilgrims and developed trust in something bigger than herself. She began to trust that things would work out for the best not only on the pilgrimage but also in her life. Changes took place within her during the journey away from the familiar, and she returned home with more than stamps on her pilgrim's passport as proof she'd walked hundreds of kilometers; she carried a transformed soul.

I'd been a sort of pilgrim too, venturing from the South of France to Egypt, India, and Switzerland, and finally deep into my secret garden where I found my soul-Self. The journey took me away and back home again to discover that I'd only needed to stay where I was, cross the threshold of my inner secret garden, and peer inside to find the answers. Many of the friends I met along the way became teachers on the journey. In a new state of calm, I wanted to remain perched in the Swiss mountains with that high vista, looking down into the valleys, watching the cars zip about below and along the river and lake. I liked being out of the fray. It felt easy to sit back and observe and stay out of the firing line. After befriending myself, it became easy to practice spiritual precepts and stay true to my values while separated from the world. I prayed about what to do and where to go next.

Ancient yogis and yoginis retreated permanently to caves and monasteries, and I wanted to do the same, but contemporary ones do not have that luxury. We're expected to get our hands dirty and bring together the sacred and the profane by rendering the world and our actions in it sacred. It's easy to say, "All is God," and see the beauty everywhere when you're alone in a mountain setting with snow-covered peaks; the sun sparkles on the snow crystals like diamonds; and an eagle soars overhead. Nature hums with divine harmony in that natural environment. But when a man I knew from high school arrived and proposed we start a relationship, I reluctantly agreed to return to an urban life in the American South. The change brought a shock that tested my commitment to my spiritual life. How can this inner work become practical and how can I apply it every day? I wondered.

At first my faith waned. I'd not achieved enlightenment as I yearned for through my asceticism and spiritual practices, but I'd acquired a firm faith that all happened in its own time and that I had more to learn and more work to do. On one of my trips to India I met a devout Indian man, Keshav, who invited me to his house at Puttaparthi. Villagers knew of him because of his huge photos of saints on the walls of his house, where nectar collected spontaneously in bowls and *vibhuti*, a sacred ash, grew on the holy images. Considered a wise man, people came to him to seek out his advice and listen to his words. An Italian friend led me to Keshav's door. His living room seemed unusually large and airy for an Indian house, and books, sacred images, and statues adorned every inch of the floors and walls. My friend hoped to learn more about his spiritual search and his yearning for a mate. But true to my American heritage of impatience and "let's-get-it-doneness," I wanted nothing less than to learn the tricks to achieving immediate enlightenment. I didn't want to go home without total and absolute self-realization. I didn't want heaven. I wanted to merge with all things right now!

"I don't want to come back again in another life," I moaned. "I want this to be it."

"You're on the right path," he said. "But so what if you have to come back? It's not a big deal."

I sighed and didn't agree. I intended to get it right this one last time and go Home with a capital H. Home to me meant merging with all I'm supposed to merge with in love and light. Deep experiences have led me to understand that reincarnation is a natural process of life. I wanted to allow my soul to grow and get off of that merry-go-round of perpetual birth and death. No more of the suffering in a physical body; no more emotional pain or seeking. I'd found the answers to my quest; now I needed to take them back and live and practice them. But as much as it irritated me, he was right. I could make efforts. In fact, I must make efforts to grow and expand, but the results would be in divine hands. The words of Jesus returned, "Not my will, but Thy will be done."

All along this journey, I'd thought I knew what was best, what I wanted, what would make me happy, and it included a deep desire for self-realization and enlightenment. My yearning for a mate transformed into a desire for a spiritual partner who would grow with me on the journey. But I didn't want to go out and look for a man. I said to the Divine, "If you want me to have a mate, you'll have to bring him here to find me. I am not going out to look!" I felt pretty sure this would be a tall order. The mountain village where I stayed contained a small population of mostly married men, a lot of dairy cows, and goats. That's when, in a huge cosmic joke, the American from high school showed up at my door, and I decided to move back to the United States to become active in the world and fully integrate the lessons I'd learned. Yet big questions remained.

How can I integrate a spiritual path with a relationship? I'm supposed to devote my life to the Divine, not to a man. But what if they were the same, and developing a relationship meant devotion to the Divine in the other? Hindus believe that all individuals should be greeted and treated as God. A houseguest, a beggar, a client, a lover. There's no difference. When we hold the intention to salute the Divine, He/She responds and benefits from the end results. But if I spent so much time with people, particularly with a mate, it would really test my devotion to seeing the Divine in all and loving all. It would bring me to accept all of the shades from darkness to light and of demon and divine in both myself and in others. It would mean more hard work.

I brooded. Yes, I wanted to move off of my mountaintop. But I didn't want to get my hands dirty in the world. What a daunting challenge! Like a child who clings to her mother's skirts and stays within her father's protective sights, I begged and pleaded to stay there in that divine comfort zone in the Swiss Alps, not fully engaged in real life, but observing, watching, amused from a mountain perch. When I returned to the U.S., I worried and asked myself, "Can the sacred and profane become one? Can I embrace it all?" On a Sunday hike in the Carolina woods, I found an answer in nature.

The sun shined clear and bright along the lakeside path, and I walked in silence with a friend among the trees sprouting with spring-green buds. Instead of a religious service, I needed nature to feed my soul. It provided all of the connection to the Divine that I needed and put me back in tune with my Self. Across the lake on this silent morning, we spotted a great blue heron perched on a tree trunk that had fallen into the water. We watched and waited, not for anything in particular, except to admire the elegant beauty of the magnificent creature with tall legs, a long thin neck, and a black and white plumed crest. It appeared larger than most of the herons we usually saw.

The great bird opened its wings and leaped to a limb above the water and leaned down in a slow, easy motion. Then, in a flash so fast that I could barely see, it captured and pulled out the biggest freshwater fish I have ever seen. The fish flopped and struggled to free itself from the bird's thin beak. The heron struggled to carry it ashore. It wobbled while the fish flapped and flailed. I doubted the bird could swallow such a huge catch. But it slowly, carefully, meticulously maneuvered the two-foot-long fish lengthwise. After about ten minutes of patient maneuvering, in one deft move the heron lifted it, held it suspended, then swallowed. Its throat stretched to several times its normal size. The thrill of watching the catch raised my spirits. The bird walked off, belly full, and found a quiet place to digest. I doubt it could have flown with all the additional weight.

What message did this synchronistic event bring? Birds represented the soul to me. The heron in particular symbolized an elevated, embodied soul. The fish was spiritual food. Jesus fed it to the masses to nourish them. The fish had also appeared in a dream in India where my mind in the form of a monkey grasped the fish tightly and would not let go. The fish represented the spirit and all that is divine. I saw the Greek fish, a symbol of spirituality, on a bumper on the way home later. It reminded me of the fish dream on the Riviera that had warned me to move. But the feeding heron appeared as a powerful symbol, a sort of waking dream scene.

"What did that mean to you?" my friend asked. He knew that sighting animals held symbolic meaning for me.

I walked in silence and contemplated for a while before answering. "Integration," I said. "It's telling me to digest and integrate all the spiritual things I've learned. The fish becomes the bird, which represents the soul. And the fish as it becomes cells, bone, and blood will fly. It's like watching the whole picture come together. The spiritual symbol plucked from the water and transformed into a beautiful heron. It means that all is one—mind, body, and spirit." I'd once perceived life as either spiritual or material, as sacred or profane, and now it's all alive with the Divine.

I realized that I'd come home to bring it all together. And now the real work began. Many dreams of guidance arrived, dreams where I perceived that all things animate and inanimate contain consciousness and "see" as we can see them. I learned to "dance" with people, to become an active part of the community with the aim to uplift and serve others through work and workshop. A big dream confirmed my feeling that my ultimate work is integration, though it didn't promise anything would be easy.

I walk in my secret garden and a bountiful pomegranate tree in the center hangs heavy with fruit. I carry a basket of pomegranates, and as I walk I see streets, office towers, nature, the world, and it's all beautiful, shimmering with light. All has transformed to become part of the secret garden, but it's no longer secret. It's no longer set apart. It's no longer just one place in an ashram in India or on a mountain peak in Switzerland. It's no longer confined to a place just inside of me. It's right here in the streets of the city. It's in the cherry blossoms, the azaleas, and the grass pushing up between the cracks in the sidewalk. People pick the pomegranates and I also share them from my basket. When the pomegranates break open, rays of light pour out. The seeds fill those who eat them with light and joy. Some people dance together in unison. The most mundane things become filled with beauty and delight. Some seeds fall and take root, creating more trees and more fruit. Soon the fruits grow everywhere, spreading peace, harmony, and joy. The secret garden is no longer just in one place. It is everywhere and everyone is in it. Nothing is set apart and all share their beautiful, soulful gifts. My secret garden transforms into a garden of bliss.

When the story began, my secret garden was little more than sand dunes in a desert. I felt small, restricted to a very limited material world, numbed out and cut off from my intuition and dreams. Separated from the deep whisperings of my soul, I almost stood on a windowsill and jumped out. But the seeds of love given to me by Karim, the Egyptian perfumer, and all of the other teachers along the way have grown into a huge tree that offers solidity, shade, protection, and peace. It took many years of commitment to that intense inner work to encourage it to grow. And the work's not done. I don't know if it ever will be. The tree continues to require constant tending through meditation, contemplation, and active work with dreams and intuition to keep it watered and alive with spiritual energy.

My secret garden has grown from a dry, restricted place to one that is verdant and flowing with vitality. It includes many, many people, places, and things and it continues to transform and expand. The lessons still come and the trials continue. But when I sometimes feel it's too much and my heart wants to close up from pain, my inner gardener whispers to me gently. "Expansion is life," she says. "Grow, my child. Grow."

As you continue to grow your secret garden, I encourage you to listen closely to your soul-Self too, for she is encouraging you to dare to continue to awaken and expand. The secret garden beckons you to come inside and join the joy on this magical adventure of the spirit. If you dare to enter and put in a little effort, you'll soon get glimpses of the joy. Eventually it stabilizes into a continual experience of bliss.

In Tune with Natural Cycles

Change is natural, like the seasons in the garden. Nothing remains static. The maple trees and roses hibernate during winter, blossom in spring, move into maturity in summer, and lose their leaves with the fall. But in life we often resist change. Our parents divorce; our kids move away; our friends take paths that send them across the globe. Companies move headquarters. Our bodies lose their flexibility and youth. Time and change go hand in hand. Welcome change. It brings opportunities. In spring it brings vibrant beauty. In summer it brings maturation. Fall brings harvest. Winter brings a time of rest and quiet.

If we go with the natural rhythm of our lives and accept change, we can make the best of it. There are periods of great activity in work and socializing, periods of introspection and solitude, and periods of growth and expansion. Sometimes when it may seem that no apparent work is being done, like in winter, the trees silently regain their forces for the coming spurt of spring. When it seems lots of physical activity may be taking place, it may instead be a sign of laziness and avoidance of exploring the inner landscape. Through a practice of acceptance and inner observation you will become aware of your own rhythms. How will you continue to tend your secret garden so that it remains vibrant and alive?

Tearing Down the Walls of Your Secret Garden

You've been exploring your inner secret garden and allowing yourself to play, dream, and invite in your inner gardener for guidance. You've had a chance to experiment, dance with the Divine, live creatively, and grow. Much of this may have been done outside of the sight of others. It's safe to start that way, but sooner or later it's time to take the spiritual self out into the world. How will you choose to tear down the walls of your secret garden? Will you first open the gate and invite others in to join you? Will you decide to volunteer or help out others in some way? Will you express your creativity and show it in public? There are many ways to move out and integrate your feminine, intuitive wisdom into the world. By listening to yourself you will know the best way to do this for you. What's the next step on your journey now?

"Ananda" means bliss or rapture ... I don't know whether my consciousness is proper consciousness or not; I don't know whether what I know of my being is my proper being or not; but I do know where my rapture is. So let me hang on to rapture, and that will bring me both my consciousness and my being.

—JOSEPH CAMPBELL

Epilogue

When the Secret Garden Becomes a Garden of Bliss

The story doesn't end with all of the strings neatly tied up in a "happily ever after" Hollywood finale. When this journey into the secret garden began several years ago, I imagined it would be neat, tidy, and rather businesslike. Follow the path and the inner guidance, and it will all come together in a smooth, easy, efficient way. But the nature of life is messy, chaotic, exquisitely beautiful, excruciatingly painful, immensely joy-filled, and unpredictable.

In the times between the beginnings of the journey on the French Riviera, the move into the Swiss Alps, the travels to Egypt and India, and the return to the American South, many happy and painful events transpired. My childhood writing dream came true and brought great joy as my first book, *Awake in the World*, appeared, won national awards, and found a home in hearts worldwide. But as one teacher said, "Life is a pleasure between two pains." Just as I'd begun to get comfortable and settle into a routine in the U.S., my world shifted again. The mate that I'd so longed for taught me many lessons, then we parted; I moved to the seaside in Charleston, grieved the loss, and had to remake a new kind of life and move more deeply into contact with my soul. In troubling times especially, I continue to return to the healing space of the inner secret garden and linger, for here I find wholeness, peace, and joy.

I don't believe the inner work ever really ends (and sometimes I feel I'd like to take a vacation!). Many heartaches, lost loves, and hurts followed that cut so deep that it seems they will never heal, but the more I dare to open and live the life that's completely in tune with my soul-Self, the less I'm able to tolerate living in the way that others expect. Living a spiritual life may not be easy. It demands total authenticity. It brings you to dance to a unique song that only you can hear fully, and sometimes you dance alone because no others can hear the music. But it offers depth, beauty, vibrancy, and a life filled with such color and creative power that it becomes impossible to go back to living in that desert of a life that existed before you lived in deep alignment with the secret gardener of the soul.

Determining to dance with your soul, your secret gardener, and maintain a sacred soul garden that's fit for her requires constant work. It demands checking in every day, every hour, and every minute to discover if the direction you want to take is her direction or the direction of some lesser aspect of yourself. I've not known anyone who commits to this work and gains an easy path in return. It's often a path fraught with doubts, challenges, and constant and regular questioning about whether where we are now is where she (the soul-Self) wills us to be.

The soul-Self doesn't follow the crowd. It encourages you to speak up when you need to and live by your truth. The way she suggested one time may not be the way she advises the next. My mind says, "Can't you tell her we need to settle down?!" It sounds insistent, whiny. But when you decide to dance with the Divine as I have, you don't question. You go with her, wherever she leads, even if it's not where your little mind imagined you'd be.

In the secret garden, the soul gardener urges and coaxes us to remain ever near her, ever in constant contact. When we move away she tears our world apart to bring us back to her again, back to our knees, kneeling at her feet in the secret garden where we can once again bathe in her light and regain inspiration, vitality, and joy. She reminds us over and over not to put too much faith in the world or in the relationships and things "out there." What counts is our life with her inside our secret garden and maintaining this peaceful inner place to return to again and again.

What I can tell you for sure is that without this inner sacred place and the contact with the soul, life would be utterly meaningless and I'd be reeling in confusion and lost in despair. Inner work that leads closer to her is all that really matters, because as it leads closer to her it leads to a more genuine life. As we live into this authentic life, the world around us becomes transformed and the people in our orbit become inspired to live more authentically, enlivened with the vibrant, energetic vitality of their own souls. Individually we may only be a drop in the ocean, but every drop counts, and eventually, together, we become the waves of change.

The trials will not end. There will not be a continually smooth road, though that road may even out some of the time. The mind, however, will become calmer as it turns more inward than out and relies more on the inner secret garden of the soul for sustenance and renewal. The inner sacred space will become richer, more textured and colorful. And the relationship with your soul-Self, your inner secret gardener who guides, tends, and gently prompts, will deepen. She will speak to you more and more through dreams, in subtle impressions, insights, and even in a still, quiet voice. She says, "Your true nature is bliss." She reminds me that when I do enough work and dig away enough junk I will live in constant awareness of my true nature. She says that I am peace, too. When the waves of pain and suffering pass through me it seems difficult to believe, but this is when faith takes over. I know she speaks truth. And so I continue to make the effort, under her vigilant guidance. She tells me that you are bliss, peace, and love, too, and that we are ultimately one, whole, and inseparable from each other. We are never isolated and alone. Your pain is my pain and mine is yours. But we also share the joy.

When things grow, friction is produced. Nothing grows smoothly and evenly. Beanstalks grow in fits and starts. Bamboo grows in quick bursts. Seeds in a garden push up the hard earth to break into the light. So it is with the growth of the soul as we grow into the light. Sometimes drought strikes. We have to push through the darkness. A storm arrives and all that we've worked for seems to be destroyed. But as in nature, the secret garden grows back vibrant and stronger than before. The challenge becomes to maintain the lightness of being, joy, and trust in the Divine even through the trying times. Careful attention to the soul-Self will reveal the ways that sustain us through the challenges and uplift us. She will coax us to grow and not fold in on ourselves and wither in darkness. Realizing the cyclical nature of life brings a certain sense of relief, and with gentle acceptance we can learn to embrace all that it offers with joy.

I cannot say that making a decision to explore your inner sacred garden of the soul will bring constant happiness and pleasure. But pleasure and happiness are different than joy. Mystic and monk Thomas Merton wrote, "And if you do not know the difference between pleasure and joy you have not yet begun to live." The nature of life, as the Buddha reminds us, is one where illness, death, departures, and separations make up part of the journey. No one will be spared some form of betrayal and loss. But joy becomes a constant when we stay connected with the inner Source. For those who choose to take a spiritual perspective, the substance and essence of life lies deeper than the physical world. It lives forever in the heart of the secret garden of the soul, and the pain of life's experiences often pushes us below the surface to rediscover the immortal soul-Self. The breath and energy of spirit animates us and we realize we cannot ever die or disappear. In this lies joy.

"The first [step] is pleasure; the second, happiness; the third is joy; and the fourth is bliss," said Indian mystic and spiritual teacher Osho in *The Dhammapada*, Volume 8. For Osho, pleasure relates to the body and physical sensations. Happiness goes a little deeper but still depends on external experiences. Joy marks the beginning of a spiritual experience associated with peace, contemplation, and contentment. It relies on a deep inner connection with the Divine and does not depend on anything outside of us, on anyone or any circumstances. Bliss is the ultimate experience. It is total, complete. "Bliss means you have reached to the very innermost core of your being," Osho said. "You start blooming when you are in tune with the whole." He continues, "Whenever you are not in tune with the whole … the whole no more nourishes you; then you are no more rooted in the whole. Then you become an uprooted tree, then you are undernourished. Then your green foliage starts disappearing. Then flowers can't happen to you, because flowers are possible only when you are over-flooded with joy, overflowing with joy."

According to the Hindu perspective, our true nature is *ananda*, which means bliss. That bliss is like the sun that always shines. It remains ever present, but the events in life and clouds of worry and even emotions like happiness may obscure it like storm clouds obscure the sun. It always amazes me when taking off from a stormy airport, how once you reach a certain altitude and get through the clouds, the sun shines as brightly as ever. If we learn to choose the experience of joy in our bodies, minds, hearts, and spirits, we will move in tune with the universe, dance in a flow of light and love, and remain above the clouds.

While in Egypt, Karim, the perfumer, aspired to create a perfume called Ananda. He said, "Joy. That is what you find in that sacred inner place. When you find it and carry it with you everywhere, then you'll know you've arrived at your destination." He aimed for his fragrance to reflect the inner joy that emanates naturally from a well-tended secret garden of the soul. It was his life's work, his aspiration to create and share his joy with others. In my dreams, too, joy becomes a constant presence. I dance in joy, dressed in red, and the sound of coins and bells accompanies me. The days pass quickly, and as I check inside to perceive the latest growth, the pomegranate tree stands firm and full of fruit. Sharing this fruit of the inner work, more than most anything else, brings deep satisfaction and immeasurable joy. As you continue to grow and expand your spirit, I wish for you that your inner secret garden will thrive and also bring you a harvest of pure bliss and the will to share your unique gifts with the world.

Creating the Fragrance of Your Life

Gardens in the South of France, where perfumery became an art, include jasmine, tuberose, lavender, and May roses. Long used in healing arts like aromatherapy, the flowers are cultivated and pressed for their precious essences. Perfumers like Karim in Egypt and Angelo in the South of France use head, heart, and base notes of the essences and essential oils to compose a fragrance. The head note is the first one detected when you smell a perfume. It gives the first impression and evaporates in a few minutes.

The heart note creates the core of the scent and lingers for several hours. It harmonizes with the head and base notes to hold the composition together. The base note is often the strongest and heaviest scent and can last for several days. When all three are blended perfectly, they create a beautiful scent. Sathya Sai Baba said, "Make your life a rose that speaks silently in the language of fragrance." Karim created Ananda as his signature perfume to represent the fragrance of his life and elicit deep feelings of joy. What will you name the fragrance you're consciously creating with your life? What will your head, heart, and base notes be? Joy, patience, compassion, love? If you feel inspired, find a beautiful bottle and label it with your perfume's name or make a collage or drawing of it to keep near you for inspiration.

Gratitude Page

In this year of many challenges and big transitions, I feel grateful to the friends, family, and colleagues who offered kind words, encouragement, and support along the way. Know that you are appreciated and loved and that your loving kindness carried me through difficult times. Special thanks to my parents for their loving support; to Carolyn Rivers for getting me to Charleston; to Nick in Val Verzasca who is like a brother to me—thank you for the quiet refuge for writing and reviving my spirit. I'm also grateful to Elizabeth Beak, who introduced me to companion planting in Charleston's urban gardens. Appreciation also goes to Llewellyn editors and to the book designers who do such a great job with layout and design. I feel special gratitude for the readers and workshop participants who explored many of these secret garden exercises with me along the way and helped me to grow. May all of your lives blossom with flowers of joy. This work is offered at the feet of the Divine, the loving source of all life. May the fruits of it be enjoyed by that Divine One.

To Write to the Author

If you wish to contact the author or would like more information about this book, please write to the author in care of Llewellyn Worldwide Ltd. and we will forward your request. Both the author and publisher appreciate hearing from you and learning of your enjoyment of this book and how it has helped you. Llewellyn Worldwide Ltd. cannot guarantee that every letter written to the author can be answered, but all will be forwarded. Please write to:

Debra Moffitt
% Llewellyn Worldwide
2143 Wooddale Drive
Woodbury, MN 55125-2989

Please enclose a self-addressed stamped envelope for reply, or $1.00 to cover costs. If outside the USA, enclose an international postal reply coupon.

GET MORE AT LLEWELLYN.COM

Visit us online to browse hundreds of our books and decks, plus sign up to receive our e-newsletters and exclusive online offers.

- **Free tarot readings** • **Spell-a-Day** • **Moon phases**
- **Recipes, spells, and tips** • **Blogs** • **Encyclopedia**
- **Author interviews, articles, and upcoming events**

GET SOCIAL WITH LLEWELLYN

Find us on Facebook
www.Facebook.com/LlewellynBooks

Follow us on twitter™
www.Twitter.com/Llewellynbooks

GET BOOKS AT LLEWELLYN

LLEWELLYN ORDERING INFORMATION

Order online: Visit our website at www.llewellyn.com to select your books and place an order on our secure server.

Order by phone:
- Call toll free within the U.S. at 1-877-NEW-WRLD (1-877-639-9753)
- Call toll free within Canada at 1-866-NEW-WRLD (1-866-639-9753)
- We accept VISA, MasterCard, and American Express

Order by mail:
Send the full price of your order (MN residents add 6.875% sales tax) in U.S. funds, plus postage and handling to: Llewellyn Worldwide, 2143 Wooddale Drive Woodbury, MN 55125-2989

POSTAGE AND HANDLING

STANDARD (U.S. & Canada):
(Please allow 12 business days)
$25.00 and under, add $4.00.
$25.01 and over, FREE SHIPPING.

INTERNATIONAL ORDERS (airmail only):
$16.00 for one book, plus $3.00 for each additional book.

Visit us online for more shipping options.
Prices subject to change.

FREE CATALOG!

To order, call
1-877-
NEW-WRLD
ext. 8236
or visit our
website

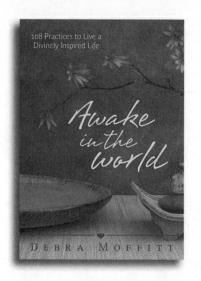

Awake in the World
108 Practices to Live a Divinely Inspired Life
DEBRA MOFFITT

Everyone needs an anchor in this fast-paced and chaotic world. *Awake in the World* offers 108 easy ways to weave soul-nourishing peace and divinity into each day.

This engaging and practical guide was inspired by the author's own personal quest for spiritual enrichment. The practices she brought back from a journey around the world changed her life—and can transform yours. Drawn from an array of wisdom traditions, these 108 bite-sized exercises—involving meditation, labyrinth walking, inspired lovemaking, mantras, and ritual—are quick and simple to do. By sharpening your spiritual awareness, you'll learn to cultivate calm in a crisis, focus on what is truly important, and recognize the divine in everyday life. To support and encourage you on this exciting journey of self-discovery, the author shares her own personal, moving stories.

978-0-7387-2722-6, 432 pp., 5 x 7   **$16.95**

Blissology

The Art & Science of Happiness

Andy Baggott

Blissology
The Art & Science of Happiness
ANDY BAGGOTT

Become the master of your own life and destiny with a simple four-step process that combines powerful law of attraction techniques, cutting-edge science, and the wisdom of some of the world's oldest spiritual traditions. We have more control over our life and our feelings than we realize, and in *Blissology*, Andy Baggott shows you how to reclaim this control and, in doing so, reclaim your power to create the life of your dreams.

This is a real, hands-on approach—you don't need to take great leaps of faith or radically change your beliefs in order to achieve a better life. Simply by using the tools and techniques within these pages, you can immediately begin to understand, practice, live, and share happiness, creating a life that is truly fulfilling and successful.

978-0-7387-2004-3, 216 pp., 5 x 7   **$14.95**

Becoming
your
Best Self

The Guide to Clarity, Inspiration and Joy

Sara
Wiseman

"Intuition is our most natural way of knowing. This book helps you return to
innate clarity and flow with easy, commonsense tips and insights. It guides you
into your truest self and life."
—Penney Peirce, author of *Frequency* and *The Intuitive Way*

Becoming Your Best Self
The Guide to Clarity, Inspiration and Joy
Sara Wiseman

At its core, intuition is a spiritual act, says Sara Wiseman—and once you understand this simple concept, psychic awakening is a given. To this end, she teaches a direct connection with the Divine that will raise your vibration, heal your heart, allow instant access to cosmic information—and transform your life in the process.

Using elegantly simple teachings and step-by-step exercises, Wiseman makes it possible for students at all levels to experience their own psychic awakening. Readers will learn a variety of life-enhancing skills, from attracting a soul mate to healing relationships through space and time to communicating with Divine guides, angels, and loved ones in spirit.

978-0-7387-2794-3, 264 pp., 6 x 9   **$16.95**

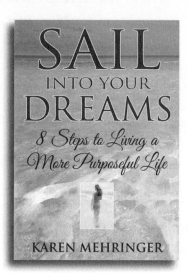

Sail Into Your Dreams
8 Steps to Living a More Purposeful Life
Karen Mehringer

Sail Into Your Dreams is the perfect book for anyone who has ever asked, "Is this all there is to life?"

Unsatisfied with her busy life in Seattle, Karen Mehringer embarked on a six-month, life-changing ocean odyssey to Australia, Indonesia, Fiji, and, most importantly, toward the joyful, fulfilling life she had always wanted.

You don't have to leave land to make your dreams come true. Karen shares the wisdom and practical tools she learned on her ocean odyssey, showing us how to focus on what truly matters. Journal entries and inspiring stories from Karen and others highlight how to slow down, nurture yourself, connect with others, and tap into your life-force energy—the source of infinite possibilities.

This eight-step program will help you assess your life and eliminate toxic relationships, emotional trauma, physical clutter, and debt—making space for new experiences that awaken your passion and spirit.

978-0-7387-1053-2, 240 pp., 5 x 7   **$13.95**

Includes 6 Steps to Success

Adrian Calabrese, Ph.D.

How to Get Everything You Ever Wanted

Complete Guide to Using Your Psychic Common Sense

How to Get Everything You Ever Wanted
Adrian Calabrese, Ph.D.

When Adrian Calabrese's faithful car bit the dust, she was broke and had already maxed out seven credit cards. She went looking for her dream car anyway, and by the end of the day she was the proud owner of a shiny Jeep Cherokee. It was all because she had found the secret formula for getting what she wanted. Not long after that, money began flowing in her direction, and she paid off all her debts and her life turned around. Now she shares her powerful method of applying ancient concepts of inner wisdom to everyday life. Starting today, anyone can begin to get everything out of life he or she desires.

978-1-56718-119-7, 288 pp., 7½ x 9⅛   **$16.95**

Dynamic Tools
to Create Change

REAL
STEPS
TO
ENLIGHTENMENT

Amy Elizabeth Garcia

Real Steps to Enlightenment
Dynamic Tools to Create Change
Amy Elizabeth Garcia

Connecting with the Divine is crucial for spiritual advancement, but choosing a spiritual path is anything but easy.

Amy Elizabeth Garcia simplifies the journey to enlightenment into thirty-three spiritual goals, such as finding your life purpose, developing trust in the universe, relinquishing the need to control, recognizing synchronicity, and fostering peace. Focusing on a specific spiritual lesson, each chapter begins with a divine message from the author's spiritual master that includes stories from his human incarnations. Garcia goes a step further in bringing these concepts to life by sharing her own life experiences. Every chapter includes a prayer inspired by angels and exercises for spiritual growth—the perfect complement to this beginner's guide to enlightenment.

978-0-7387-0896-6, 264 pp., 5³⁄₁₆ x 8   **$14.95**

"An expansive and comprehensive manual that will help you understand your soul's purpose. I highly recommend this book."
— BRIAN L. WEISS, MD, author of *Many Lives, Many Masters*

SoulVisioning

Clear the Past, Create Your Future

SUSAN WISEHART

Soul Visioning
Clear the Past, Create Your Future
SUSAN WISEHART

This groundbreaking book teaches you how to create a life of passion and purpose by following your soul's wisdom. Using breakthrough methods such as energy psychology (acupuncture for the emotions without the needles), guided journeys, forgiveness practices, and past-life and life-between-lives regression, you'll discover practical, step-by-step techniques to heal the unconscious beliefs that block the awareness of your true spiritual identity and life purpose.

The soul-visioning journey connects you with your Higher Self to guide you into the ideal expression of your soul in your work, relationships, health, finances, and spirituality. Powerful and inspiring case examples with long-term follow-up interviews demonstrate the remarkable results that Wisehart's clients have experienced from these life-changing techniques.

978-0-7387-1408-0, 336 pp., 6 x 9   **$17.95**

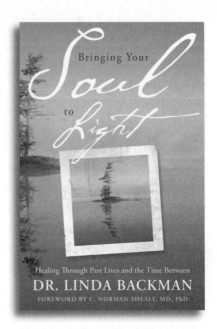

Bringing Your

Soul

to

Light

Healing Through Past Lives and the Time Between

DR. LINDA BACKMAN

FOREWORD BY C. NORMAN SHEALY, MD, PhD

Bringing Your Soul to Light
Healing Through Past Lives and the Time Between
DR. LINDA BACKMAN

What happens after we die? What is the purpose of my current life? Have I lived before?

In this unique and inspiring guide, Dr. Linda Backman answers these questions with compassion, objectivity, and more than thirty years of experience conducting traditional and past-life regression therapy with clients. *Bringing Your Soul to Light* includes a wealth of firsthand accounts from actual past-life and between-life regression sessions, offering readers a compelling and personal glimpse into the immortality of the soul.

You will discover the extraordinary universal connections we all share in this lifetime and beyond. You'll learn how you can use this knowledge to heal and grow, both physically and spiritually, by understanding yourself on a soul level and releasing energetic remnants of past-life trauma. *Bringing Your Soul to Light* includes a foreword by holistic healing pioneer and author C. Norman Shealy, M.D., Ph.D.

978-0-7387-1321-2, 264 pp,. 6 x 9   **$16.95**